Unlocking Wealth!

Unlocking Wealth is not intended, and I hope that it will not be used as an authoritative source. It's more on the line of concepts and principles, as well as a guide. What I believe as we head into the new millennium, is that more and more consumers will be in great need of help financially. The concepts and principles that have been used in the past will not be effective.

Churches are teaching prosperity. It is the concepts and principles that are not being understood. What we are trying do is to go back to the foundation that promises prosperity to all. By establishing the Word of God as the foundation, I believe that many people's financial lives will change. And perhaps, a new definition for wealth will be formed. Beginning with these seven principles:

Biblical Principles. Understanding God's foundation in dealing with money, and that our ability to get wealth is by his power.

Sound Judgment. Using the foundation of biblical principles to make judgment.

Determine Goals. Your ability to use sound judgment to establish your goals.

Budgeting. Managing your goals within a controlled environment.

Relationship. Understanding the need of a sound relationship with your money and your bank.

Eliminate Liability. To reduce your debt simply by understanding the processes of accumulation of interest.

Secure and Develop Assets. Knowing what assets are and the need to develop them as you eliminate debt. Securing it with foundation products.

i

Wealth Accumulation Concepts
P. O. BOX 109
Marietta, Georgia 30061

©2002 By Robert Wilson

All rights reserved. Published in the United States
by Wealth Accumulation Concepts Atlanta, Georgia

Library of Congress Catalog Number:
ISBN   0-9721065-0-2

Wilson, Robert
Unlocking Wealth
www.unlockingwealth.com

04   03   02   01   00   5   4   3   2   1

Manufactured and Printed in the United States of America

TABLE OF CONTENTS

Chapter I   Spiritual Laws of Money

Chapter II   Personal Wealth Building Education

Chapter III   Budget Planning

Chapter IV   Financial Trouble

Chapter V   Doing It For Yourself

Chapter VI   Credit

Chapter VII   About Student Loans

Chapter VIII   Mortgages

Chapter IX   Bill Collectors

Chapter X   Wage Garnishment

Chapter XI   Letters To Use

Chapter XII   Your Power

I have known Robert Wilson since 1998 as a member of Word of Faith Family Worship Center. The revelation that God has given him concerning finance is so desperately needed in the body of Christ. This book will help you understand some financial principles that will put you on the path to financial freedom and prosperity. The bible says "my people are destroyed for a lack of knowledge." For many years, people have given their lives to Christ, have served Him with all of their heart, have operated in the gifts of the Spirit, but had no knowledge of financial principles. This book was written for such a time as this because many ministers are preaching a prosperity message around the world. I truly believe that it is God's will that we prosper. I also believe that preparation is the key to success.

Today many of us are not blessed financially because we are not prepared to deal with the increase. Reading, understanding, and applying the principles contained in these pages will help open up the floodgates of prosperity in your life. For many years, the only thing we heard about finances were tithes and offerings. Robert Wilson is addressing not only the tithe, but also how to handle the other 90% of your income.

Many of us do not need an increase of our income until we have the wisdom to know what to do with the 90% that God has placed in our trust. James wrote, "if any of you lack wisdom, let him ask of God, that giveth to all men liberally and upbraideth not." Wisdom is more valuable than rubies. Wisdom will bring increase in your life. Wisdom is knowing what to do next. Many people in the body of Christ have no idea how to handle their finances. Consequently, they make some imprudent decisions concerning their money. Wisdom is the practical application of the knowledge that you have received and understood.

This book will help you get an understanding of basic financial principles so that you can apply it to your life. Mike Murdock said, "If you want something you've never had, you must do something you've never done." I want you to ask yourself the question, "Am I a good steward over my finances?"

In order for God to increase us financially, we must be good stewards over the money we presently have. Excellence is doing the best you can on the level that you are. You cannot graduate to college if you cannot pass high school. Some people have been kept back in the financial school of their lives because they refused to learn. It is time for you to learn and move to the next level. The Bible teaches us that if we will be faithful over little, God will make us ruler over much.

This is a conditional statement, which means if you don't do the first part then you are disqualified to receive the second part. The first part is being faithful over little. Remember God is moved by our faith and not necessary by our moaning, complaining, and crying. Without faith it is impossible to please God. Your faithfulness in what you have right now will propel you into a land flowing with "milk and honey" or "silk and money." Why will god trust you with a $100,000.00 income and you cannot manage a $20,000.00 income. If you are not tithing on the $20,000.00 income, then don't deceive yourself to think that you will tithe on a $100,000.00 income.

Have you ever thought about how an athlete or entertainer could make millions of dollars, but still have to file for bankruptcy? It is because when they were making minimum wage, they had no concept of financial stewardship. Sometimes our talent takes us where our character cannot keep us. I believe we are a testimony of the character of God when we are good stewards over our finances.

Remember that God promotes faithfulness. When we are faithful over that which is another man's, God will give you that which is your own. When you are faithfully paying rent and taking care of someone else's property you are setting yourself up to be blessed with a home of your own. When you are faithful as an employee on a job, you are setting yourself to be blessed with your own business. God has given every man and woman a measure of faith. That means that you have no excuse, but you have everything you need to do what needs to be done. Many times while we are waiting on God, God is actually waiting on us. Your faithfulness is a key to financial freedom and prosperity.

Another key to financial freedom and prosperity is the principle of sowing and reaping. You must understand that we gain by trading. We have gained eternal life because Jesus Christ traded his life for ours. You must invest to increase. The greatest investment you could make is in the kingdom of God.

Robert Wilson not only discusses the principle of tithing, but also teaches us to invest in our future through many means such as IRA's, mutual funds, cds stocks, etc. It is not enough just to tithe the 10% of our increase; we must also do something with the 90% that is left. Many Christians today live for tomorrow, we are very shortsighted concerning finances.

However, a good man leaves an inheritance to his children's children. The principles in this book will help get you on the path to financial perpetuity. Where not only will you be blessed but also your grandchildren will reap the benefits of your life. It was really hard for me to come to the understanding that I must lose something before I gain. I had a real problem in investing and releasing what was in my hands. I had to understand that whatsoever I doeth shall prosper; and if I didn't do anything then I am not in a position to prosper. If you want God to breathe upon your life, you must not only do something with your gifts and talents, but you must also do something with your finances.

Don't go and bury your finances like the man that had one talent. In reading this book you will discover ways that you can do something with your finances so that when you appear before God he will say "Well done thy good and faithful servant." Be blessed and enjoy your road to financial freedom and prosperity!!!

Rev. Reginald Garmon
Assistant Pastor- Word of Faith Family Worship Center

ACKNOWLEDGEMENTS

In the course of writing this book, there were many moments when I had to dig deep inside and I would like to acknowledge what and whom I found there. There is GOD: the only thing greater than myself. His grace and his mercy have become more evident in my life. In all of my years of knowing and reading the Word of God, he has now revealed himself. To Him be all glory and honor for any wisdom that you may find in this book. Next, there are two powerful men of God, Bishop Victor P. Smith and Pastor Dale C. Bronner, my spiritual Father and Shepard that were used by God to guide and encouraged me.

Then the wisdom of both of my beloved parents, each of them has left a mark within me that I cannot put into words. There is my wife Jennifer, who encouraged me and erased self-doubts after I felt this book would not happen. My son Carlos, who constantly challenges me to be a great father, a daddy, and a friend. And then as I looked inside of me, I found my friends: Guy and Lena, Peter and Janice, Daryl and Gail, Pamela, Tony, Mike, Milton, Steve, and so many more, that a part of each of them is within me. They say you are what you eat, I have received something from each of them. Thank you all.

I would also like to extend my appreciation to those who directly have aided in my business development and the publication of this book. Nathaniel H. Bronner, Jr. who has been a mentor to me in business sharing his valuable knowledge. C. W. Copeland for teaching me the value of relationships. Rev. Reginald Garmon who quietly persuade you to move forward. Marian Barnes with the incredible ability to listen with fairness. Carise Mason for her help in editing. Also, to the Nathaniel H. Bronner, Sr. Entrepreneur Center founders Ron, Marian, Monica, Charles, Steve, Milton, Phyllis, Kathy, Shirley, George, Cathy, and Johnetta. Each of them has taught me patience in the final weeks of this book. But, most importantly they have tolerated me.

Unlocking wealth in the new millennium was immeasurably improved by the insightful comments of those who read and edited the manuscript. I would like to thank Gwen Trahan for the sacrifices she made to jump right on this and meet the dead line. Also, Wanda, Teresa, Allison, Marvin, and Martin for their input.

Last but not least, special thanks are due to many people in the radio industry that have provided me the chance to share great words of encouragement directly to the general public. First, to Connie Flint who believes that information is power in the black community and has allowed me to give consumers this knowledge by way of radio, Rev. Lorraine Jacques-White the host of the radio talk show Ministerial Insight exclusively on WAOK 1380 AM in Atlanta, GA. Her skill, enthusiasm, and energy have allowed me to become a houschold name in the credit and financial field on radio. I cannot forget the late Mr. Leonard Tippy Calloway who was the number one gospel radio announcer in the world for his spin on music, life, and the fun that you must have with every thing that you do.

I could write a monster of a book, just about what all of my family, friends and business acquaintances really mean to me, but for now, I want to say **Thanks To You All.**

Robert Wilson

INTRODUCTION FROM THE AUTHOR...

Power, what does it really mean? Without going to your dictionary, ponder in your mind for its true meaning. For years, I always thought that it was being dominate over others, or just having a lot of money, allowing you to have control. I thought it was having strength and being able to overtake the position of an opponent. Am I alone in thinking this way? Well, I want to give you power, or reveal your power to you.

There are many products that offer information on finances. Regretfully, much of it is the same things you here over and over, not really dealing with practical resolutions. I want to give you the power. I remember a game I used to play as a child. It was a repeat after me game. Let's play it. I say "You remind me of the man" You say "what man"? I say, "the man with the power", you say, "what power"? I say, "the power of you do", you say, "who do" I say, "yes, you do remind me of the man", and so on.

Who is this man with the power? It is you. The power that controls your own destiny is within your own understanding. When I first looked at the meaning of the word power I was truly amazed at what it said. Power is the ability and the capacity to act or perform effectively. That was not enough for me, so I wanted the meaning of ability, capacity, act, perform, and effectively also. Ability = Skill. Capacity = The ability to receive, hold, or absorb. The maximum amount that can be contained. Act = To perform in a dramatic production. To behave. Perform = Accomplish. Fulfill. Effectively = Having an intended or desired effect.

Having skills with the income in your home is your ability. Receiving the knowledge and absorbing a plan of action is your capacity. To behave, and perform dramatically is how you are to act.

You cannot build wealth without using a fundamental process. Capacity, ability, act, perform, and effectively are just a few of the principles that you will learn as we take this journey. I want you to receive the full effect of true real life experiences and actual happenings that will empower you. I want to empower you with ideas that will help you accomplish your goals. Finally, I hope that the extensive research and the dedication that you will find in this book will first and foremost save you money and provide you the knowledge that you will benefit from for the rest of your life.

Robert Wilson

CHAPTER ONE

SPIRITUAL LAWS OF MONEY

As I was writing this book I had many different experiences about the nature or the principle in dealing with money. I first thought that there were just a few areas that have a spiritual nature. I later learn that all principles in dealing with finances or money are spiritually related regardless of any faith. While at the same time money is spiritually valueless, it cannot provide spiritual salvation. I would like to point out that this chapter was revised not to offend or alienate any group of people. Also, not to compromise my beliefs in the divine purpose of prosperity and it's spiritual laws.

When a man love and trust in the spiritual laws of prosperity, he realize that it is not a name it or claim it opportunity. Spiritual laws clearly give us conditions that we must honor. By honoring those conditions, we can experience a rich fill life with no sorrow. If we think about our relationships or divine purpose with money, and truly evaluate where our heart is, there we may find our riches.

As you consider debt relief and wealth, you must consider what your relationship is with money. We are either consumed with getting rich or fighting not to be poor. Often times there is not a middle of the road. As you look at particular areas that affect your thinking and what you do in order to accumulate riches, you may find that it is not as attractive as you imagined. There can be long-term affects and consequences of managing or mismanaging money without spiritual understanding.

Just today, while doing research for the section, I was listening to the local evening news. They spoke of a tragic incident where a man had risked his life saving in the stock market and suffered a major loss. He went home and killed his wife of thirty years and his three children (the youngest was 14 months old) than shoot himself. This was a great loss, the great loss was innocent lives. Understand spiritual laws of money, stories like this would not happen. Yet, they are as common as the one percent of the wealthiest people in the world.

On the other hand, I sit down recently with a millionaire that really understands the spiritual laws of money. He pointed out how fulfill his life is with the simplicity of life itself. I thought (yea right) it's easy to say that when you have money. Immediately as if he anticipated my thoughts, he concluded by saying for many who have had wealth lost it only because they sought a grander life. By seeking a grander life, the simple things are lost. By understanding the spiritual laws of money, it indicates the insight that is involved with having prosperity.

That opens a door of thinking, insight being a spiritual law. Having insight is a major high for those who have found it. Imagine being on a dark path to nowhere, not knowing what maybe ahead of you. Because of the darkness, your approach is with caution and perhaps even fear. Suddenly, you are able to see, as if someone has turn on a light to guide you down the path. Spiritual insights provide a different view of your decision-making and dealings. It is a spiritual knowledge that works within you waiting for the light to be turned on. It is per-sonal, it relates to the things that involve your life today as well as in the future. Spiritual insights develop outwardly as we engage it with ideas, concepts and identifying things that are honorable. Even when we have fear and doubt in ourselves we can rely on the spiritual insight to step in and guide us.

How profound is "simple?" Is it really just that simple? Insight pro-vides us with what is important for us to know and understand. Just to see clearly in our decision making, regardless of the moment in time.

Yet, insight is truly not enough, it develops experience. Each of us has a different personal history and background that has different level of understanding. With these different levels we will act differently in the decision making process. These decisions should be based on the level of insight that we have.

If you are not able to afford something our insight should engage us with a spirit of conviction before we make a decision to purchase it. Experience can be learned from observing the outcome of what other my directly experience. That my very well be the light being turn on for us, we all shall have experiences that are common in life. These experiences are important for our growth spiritually.

We all will make a financial mistake that will embarrass us. But, the experience from that mistake should give us the insight to correct that mistake in the future. It should also be shared with others to provide them the understanding of the mistake that was made. This also opens up another door of the spiritual laws of money. Giving, this I will talk about later. With insight and using our experiences we can become a closer to a divine purpose.

There is a story that I was taught growing up in the church, that story had very little meaning to me then. Maybe, because I was not concern at the time or I did not understand. Today really believe that I did not understand, there were not experiences there to draw upon. You may have heard or read it yourself, if not I shall tell this story in my own words.

There was a king who was about to travel on a long journey. Prior to leaving he decided to give to his servants money according to their abilities. This king was known for his accountability of all that he owned. They all knew that in business he took all that he could, even if it was not his.

Before he left on his travel he to one servant $5000.00 and to another $2000.00 and to another $1000.00, each according to his own ability.

The story states that the king had been gone for a number of years, and in the meantime the servants acted accordingly. The first went out and did business according to his ability. In doing business, he had doubled his king's money. The second likewise did good business that he was able to double his money. Now, the third now the heart of the king felt that it was necessary that he not take a chance with this money. So, he got a can and buried the money.

When the king return, his first servant came to him saying master you left me with five and I have gain you five more. The king was proud and thanked his servant by saying he was faithful over little he gave him more. He then welcomes him to enjoy the happiness of the king. His second servant likewise did he give honor to. But, when the third servant arrives he said to him king I know how accountable you are, and how you take from where you have not labored. So, I refused to take a chance and lose your money I buried it to keep it safe from loss. The king took back his money, and said that if you knew how accountable I am, and how I take from where I have not labored, you could have deposited it with a banker and I could have earn interest. The king in anger said to his servant you are lazy, unfaithful and worthless depart from me.

This story has all of the spiritual laws of money within it. I am sure that you have picked up on some of them already. I want to talk about just a couple of them for this chapter. First, is each of them had they own abilities. Their abilities came about though their experiences and insight to do business. Like each of you, will find that your abilities are personal to you according to your experiences and insight. Therefore do not confuse what other may obtain to what you may have. Your abilities will allow you to increase or decease according to how you engage them. As the first two servants they had vision because of their insight and the experiences they were able to draw from.

The third servant also had the insight and the experiences to draw from and may have had more. But, because of fear, he operated without any vision and without relying on the insight and experience he had.

Many times we operate outside of the knowledge that we have that gets us in financial trouble. Fear will depress the spiritual insight that is within you. It will break down your guidance system and prevent you from growing and developing yourself. As you will see in the following chapters how many of our decision to fulfill our lives are more complicated than they should be. We seek after things that do not bring value "interest" back to us.

Second, again the first two servants had use stewardship in the process as well. Even with all of the insight and experiences it is important to be great steward over that you have. Stewardship is a spiritual term meaning caretaker. You must become and caretaker over the things that you have or is given. Your accountability is measured on how will you handle things within your control. It is not foreseeable that a person, who came not handle or manage something small, can take care of something much larger. Often, we want more when we are not able to manage the little that we have. We always seem to think that if we had just a little more we could do so much better.

I remember taking a trip to my hometown, I was involved in a conversation that really got me upset. One of the people that I was talking to made a statement that shows the level of understanding that a lot of people have. She said that when she "gets some money" she would like to save and invest. I ask her why not begin to save now? She replied, I am living paycheck to paycheck now. How can I save? This was my opportunity to deliver, I ask her a few question about what she was doing with her money.

In short this is what she said. I live with my mom so I do not have to pay for rent. I do help with groceries, and some of the bills. My biggest expense is my car payment it eat up two-thirds of the money I bring home. So I cannot save money now, I even have money going to my savings account each time I get paid.

This is not the effort of stewardship, this is a false effort consumed with fear. She has no vision to understand that while not having to pay rent or a mortgage payment it is a great opportunity to save money. Her limited insight was her ability to only look at how good she looked in her late model car. Already in a process of saving money, she misused it weekly instead.

After turning on her spiritual insight lights she was able to begin to look at other areas that she was mismanaging her income. The saving that she was doing is now redirected to a CD that has a compounding daily interest rate. She refuses to give up the car now, but is starting to reorganize how she manages her current income before seeking more.

There are so many people trying not to be poor, and they are creating poverty in their own lives by live outside their means. False efforts not only depresses your spiritual insight it also destroys the fabric of the spiritual laws of money. Our spiritual guidance system helps us to grow in all areas of our lives, we have to engage it constantly in order for it to work.

Turn on your lights, that spiritual insight that is within you. Become an engager of your dreams with ideas, concepts and identify the things that will cause your insight to grow. Another aspect in the spiritual laws of money is the emotional affect that will both build and increase your insight. Or, it will like fear chew away at the fabric of your guidance system.

We must always face our emotion honestly and personally our emotions are valid. The way we feel, think, act, and do is driven by how we deal with financial decision emotionally. Arguably, the ultimate test of most marriages is the emotional side of making financial decision. Having the feelings of guilt, anger, and humiliation block the spiritual laws of money.

Our society has successfully created a social system that measures you by what you have or do not have. What you get out of spending in this type of system is the judgment of others. We emotionally seek the approval, disapproval, admiration, and contempt of other on how we are making or what we are doing with money.

There is nothing wrong with having fine things as long as they are not the things that define who you are. Consider the fact that if you had as much money as you desires, living in a prestige neighborhood, driving a fine car, and having fine jewelry you may be consider a superior person. The other side of that is if you do not have the money needed you may be judged as inferior.

The emotional side of dealing with money can eat away at you. That is why, you must develop the spiritual laws of money. Understanding that there are areas that will need to be focus on within you. Unlock yourself, turn on the lights, and use your experiences to overcome the false values that society has created. Share with others the spiritual insight of your emotion and watch how well you grow.

Emotional attachments are normally the hardest to deal with. As you grow in the spiritual laws, you will find that your old attachments will simply fall off. Even in marriages, the debates, distrust, and confusion will begin to vacate the premises. You will be able to give more to yourself, your marriage, and your financial responsibilities. Giving is the next law that I would like to talk about.

We have all heard that it is better to give than receive. But when it appears that you can barely make it, that is when giving becomes a test of all of the spiritual laws. Giving provides you with a since self worth, yet to the receiver it is a since of encouragement. Giving is not always easy to do, at first it can be a challenge. But, once you have overcome that challenge, life elevates to a new level.

There are many form of giving under the spiritual laws of money. It is not just money, it is anything that could be a value to someone else. You should not give looking for a quick return. Your giving should be as one who would plant a seed of corn. I like the cycle of a single kernel of corn, it is so encouraging once your understand it's reproduction.

If you took one single kernel of corn and planted in good soil and watered it properly. It will reproduce one stalk with four ears of corn. Each ear of corn could have about 132 kernels each. If you lost half to the weather or it was consumed, you are left with 264 kernels to replant. The same process is repeated and in the second year of harvest without any loss the 264 plants reproduces 1056 ears of corn, with 139,392 kernels to replant. There is a lot of giving and labor in this process, but the reward is plentiful.

Likewise, when you give of yourself, your time, your energy, your kindness, or your money. There will become a time of harvest. Because, when you give or plant something, it is a flow of implantation. The natural response to implantation is that what you have giving or planted begin to germinate.

Once, germination begins or take root, it will sprout up and grow to reproduce that which is giving or planted. There two important considerations that you must make. The first is to use your experience to guide you in giving. Like planting, you just can't not plant a seed anywhere. You must know that the soil that you place your seed in is fertile. The choices with what you do with your time, your energy and/or your money require the same.

Many of you may know someone who has participated and lost hard earn money in a scam called friends helping friends. Whether it was friends helping friends or some other type of networking scam, it was not fertile soil.

Next, is applying your spiritual insight that allows you to have a vision of what you want to accomplish. The spiritual insight will help you remain focus on your goal. Remember, it is your guiding light. Having your lights on allows you see the turns and stop signs ahead.

If there is ever a need to detour to avoid a serious loss ahead, that is when spiritual insight is at its best.

In the next Chapter, you will begin to look at what you are doing and considering why you are doing it that way. We want to unlock your ability to make sound financial decision. There is a great level of distance from being debt free and experiencing financial freedom.

IT PLEASES GOD
TO BLESS YOU RICHLY,
WITHOUT SORROW.

Rob Wilson

CHAPTER TWO

PERSONAL WEALTH BUILDING EDUCATION

In this chapter, we would like to examine some of the various styles that affect the way a person manages finances, or, allow the power of money to control them.

Thousands of Americans are carrying huge debt loads. If you have taken on more debt than you can handle, don't be discouraged. You are not alone. It does not matter how much money you make, where you live or whom you know. If you cannot live within your means, you are a slave to your creditors. You must learn to master your money instead of letting it master you. The love and mismanagement of money can destroy you if you let it. Examine your reasons about why you are in debt. I am not referring to financial hardship caused by things you cannot control.

So you want to change how you handle money, create a financial portfolio or even invest? Wealth building requires careful planning and consideration. As you already know, without proper planning, spending can have a drastic affect on building wealth. Before you begin considering building wealth there are things that we must identify with. One of those things will be to define what wealth truly is. I do not intend to damper your belief system, perhaps just enlighten you.

As stated in the author's thoughts regarding the first definition of the word power, you will see just how the meaning easily relates to money. Examining problems in all areas of planning, budgeting, saving, investing, and insurance products will have to be dealt with. Before an effective financial management or wealth building program can be implemented, these areas will need to be identified and dealt with.

At each level of the process to build wealth, we examine the styles of money management or mismanagement. There are probably hundreds of different styles and ways for which a person handles their money. We came up with six ways to examine in this book. As you read further, you may find that more than one of these styles may fit the way you deal with money. Many would be savers or investors are scared away because of a process they feel is complex and intimidating. By providing you with clear and consistent information we hope to minimize and eliminate any fear.

Sharing information on some of the ways people deal with money management, and their finances may help you understand what you are doing with your money. What are some of the different styles of money management? We are going to provide you with the ones that I am familiar with first hand. Without considering myself first, I looked at a few of my best friends. Who do you know, that has one of these types of styles of dealing with money? But, when I considered myself, I had to go back to really identify my style. So, if you do not find your style here in this book, it will be important for you to examine yourself.

Bargain Boomers

Bargain boomers are people that will purchase almost anything if they believe it is a good deal. Most bargain boomers are willing for an item because it is priced at $19.95 a month, without even considering the total cost. These items, in most cases, are items that they have very little use for.

• Why don't you have enough self-control to buy later or never?
• Why do you buy items that you do not use?

I Will Take It

I will take it, is just that. Because of their inability to resist pressure by friends, family, and salespersons they just cannot say no. Just saying no is more difficult to do when you are up against some of the strategies that are employed today.

• Who is telling you that you have to live high on the hog?
• What is so hard about saying no?

That's For Me

That's for me. I know it has my name on it. Can you see me in that dress, suit, car, or house? That was really made just for me. Giving in to the many different advertisements, they purchase items for their appeal. The appeal may be a need or simply a want.

• What is it that compels you to buy that item right now?
• If it just for you, why is it that others have it also?

The Jones'

Okay, we all know the Jones. They require, if not demand, the same products and lifestyle of their friends and neighbors. Often times the items or products normally cost more than they can afford. They pattern their lifestyles after others, their clothes, household items, car, and home just to name a few.

• Do you feel you have to compete financially with your friends, coworkers, neighbors, and family?
• Are you trying to impress someone?

Make Me Feel Good

Make me feel good, I am depressed, unhappy, angry, worried, and anxious. I need to spend money. This person finds relief for their emotional state of mind by spending money. Like any of the other styles, spending money without considering the cost.

• Do you buy stuff to mask your own insecurities?
• Are you using money as a drug to comfort yourself?

Oops, Let's Go Shopping

Oops, let's go shopping. Hey look I've got credit cards. They just came in the mail. I do not have to pay for at least thirty days. This person normally has access to money, credit cards, and credit line without supervision or guidance.

• Can you really pay for it?
• I know, money really burns your pockets. Right?

How amazing it is to consider the small things that control our emotions. Our styles are in many ways brought on through the initial desire from the heart. As we look ahead, you may question your own styles. I hope that you will, because if you do, you may find that your style has a dramatic affect on your goals. And if you intend to build wealth, you must have a sense of your identity, your style and your purpose.

"These are serious styles and questions, which must be answered before you can attempt to control your money. Regardless of the budget or financial system you choose. On the other hand, consider cancer growth gone untreated, it can cause death."

How To Budget Your Way And Become Debt Free

Now that you've reviewed some of the personal styles and reasons people find themselves in debt, let's look at some drastic measures to attack debt. It's time to develop a plan to determine where all of your money is going. While considering your style, we want to develop a healthy financial plan. You must be able to account for every penny you spend each month. Wait! Don't worry. You won't have to cut your spending, at least not yet. Here's a simple method to develop a plan to fit your comfort zone:

Step 1

Use the budget form on page 18, we will call it the "Financial Data." This is where you will list all your relatively fixed expenses (mortgage/rent, telephone, electric, water, tithes, gas, car, credit card minimums, etc.)

Step 2

This may seem to be the tough part. You will have to estimate how much you spend on variable expenses like food, eating out, entertainment, items for the house, school, clothing, car repair, gasoline, etc. One of the ways to determine these expenses is to track your spending. Write down everything you spend money on. Create different categories like entertainment, household, personal care, car repair, etc.

If you come across an item that doesn't fit into any one category, make the decision and pick one. For now, magazine subscriptions will go in the "Entertainment" category. Track your spending wherever you go. If you spend money, write it down. Be very detailed with your categories. This must be done for a complete month.

For example, one category might be **"Personal Care."** Under this heading write down the date, description, and the dollar amount each time you are provided the service.

PERSONAL CARE

DATE	ITEM	AMOUNT
5/1/99	Finger Nails	$20.00
5/10/99	Wash & Set	$40.00
5/25/99	Wash & Set	$40.00
5/31/99	Finger Nails	$20.00

This format allows you to see exactly where all of your money is going. If you don't know where your money is going, how can you expect to control it?

Step 3

After tracking all of your expenditures for one month, total each category, and you'll see exactly how much you are spending on everything. You may be shocked to realize how much you spend on little things. For example, if you spend $20.00 on nails and $40.00 on hair twice a month, you will spend $120 per month on those items alone. **After you've totaled your categories, transfer them and their respective expense totals to your "Financial Data" on page 21.**

Step 4

List your take home income after taxes on your "FINANCIAL DATA." You may find that one pay period usually is tighter than the other because you have to pay your bigger bills like, mortgage/rent, car payments, etc. Later, we will develop two different budgets based on the total household budget to work with your pay periods.

Step 5

It could be challenging to balance your income and expense categories, to stay within your budget. Take a long hard look at your variable expenses and see how you can reduce them. Look at a category like "Entertainment" which may include dinners out, movies, movie rentals, plays, etc.

Let's say you're currently spending $55 per week on eating out and entertainment. That's $220 per month. When you look at personal care also, the combined total is $340. Why not reduce the combine cost and look to save. We will cover this in more detail later.

You'll have to play around with the amounts you set for your variable expenses categories. You don't want to completely cut out your fun. I know you feel it's hard already, do not give up on budgeting. You will have to adjust, adjust, and adjust as you go.

Step 6

By now, your "Financial Data" should list everywhere your money goes. When you start living out your new budget, you find that it is really not that hard. You will see next how simply you can make this really work for you and your family.

Think of it this way, this is the road to financial freedom. The power of money is now in your control. Every dollar you spend must be deducted from its appropriate account balance. What you'll find is that you have money left over at the end of your budget period.

Revisit your Financial Data and adjust it accordingly. I hope these tips have encouraged you. Good luck on pursuing financial freedom!

FINANCIAL DATA SHEET

Salary: Weekly $_____   Bi-Weekly $_____   Monthly $_____

Other Income_____ Total Net Income_____

Rent/Mortgage	$ _____		
Sewer	$ _____	Household	$ _____
Water	$ _____	Saving	$ _____
Lights	$ _____		
Gas	$ _____	**Credit Card/Other Debt**	
Cable	$ _____	**Monthly Payments**	
Telephone	$ _____		
Food Expenses	$ _____	_____ $_____	
Child Care	$ _____	_____ $_____	
Clothing Expenses	$ _____	_____ $_____	
Health	$ _____	_____ $_____	
Life	$ _____	_____ $_____	
Auto	$ _____	_____ $_____	
Car Payment	$ _____	_____ $_____	
Taxes	$ _____	_____ $_____	
Church Tithes	$ _____	_____ $_____	
Personal Care	$ _____	_____ $_____	
Gasoline Exp.	$ _____	_____ $_____	
Alimony	$ _____	_____ $_____	
Child Support	$ _____	_____ $_____	
Home/Rent Ins.	$ _____	_____ $_____	
Personal Care	$ _____		
Club Fees	$ _____	Total Income $_____	
Entertainment	$ _____	- Total Debt $_____	
		=Remaining $_____	

First you must get a total of all income that it constant. After you have totaled all of your expense subtract them from the total income and you will have what is remaining. This portion of income is what you will use to eliminate debt or build wealth, depending what goals you set.

Identify Expenses *(wants vs. needs)*

I know you thought that we were finished with budgeting. We are really just beginning. This is so important if we fail in this area it is over. You need to know your current financial condition. Looking at your financial statement will give you a clear understanding and assessment of your condition. I also know that we have not talked about a financial statement, at least not directly.

A financial statement consists of three areas of budgeting; income & expenses, balance sheet, and your financial ratios. Let me take a moment to expand on each of them to allow you the ability to understand how they work together.

You just finished reading about setting up a budget. An income and expense statement is part of what you read about. It allows you to examine where you were or headed and to see how you have spent or can spend. It will also consist of any net gains or losses once you subtract your income from your expenses. The balance sheet provides an overview of your current financial condition. A person can examine the overall situation. The balance sheet provides your net worth by taking all of your liabilities from your assets. Assets are the total value of the things you own.

Liabilities are just the opposite. They are the things you owe. And finally, financial ratios are information taken from income & expenses, and balance sheets. You can calculate your ratios and determine what your percentages are. Debt to income ratio or debt to asset ratios is commonly used.

As we talk about identifying expenses (wants vs. needs) I would like to say this, taking control does not mean giving up. Before you can truly make a financial decision, you should give a lot of thought to what really constitutes a need versus a want. This will help you make rational decisions about money.

Many financial consultants agree in principal about wants vs. needs, but there are areas where we differ. As an example, some will recommend that you try to reduce your expenses. Reducing your expenses may result in reducing the quality of your life as well. Take a close look at the following.

- **Cut out any unnecessary spending such as eating out, expensive entertainment and avoid impulse purchases.**
- **Consider taking public transportation rather than owning a car.**
- **Clip coupons, purchase generic products,**
- **Stop incurring new debt.**
- **Consider substituting a debit card for your credit cards.**
- **Use your savings and other assets to pay down debts.**
- **Withdrawing savings from low-interest accounts to settle high-rate loans.**
- **Selling off a second car not only provides cash but also reduces insurance and other maintenance expenses.**

Consider what these changes could really make in your household. But before you do, let us see if there is another way to obtain the same results. Remember, we are not looking for a quick fix, we want power over our money.

Now, here is what I have to offer you. Let's use the three P's (**provide, protect, and preserve**) as our foundation as we go though this section.

The three P's provide you with the knowledge to effectively manage your money, work within a set budget, protecting you and your family's credit rating, assets, and financial reputation. Preserving the essence of your way of life, your credit, and financial future. Anything short of this will only compromise your way of life.

Remember, this a financial wealth building map, there will be different roads to choose from. As you learn more about the "Financial Data," this will all make since.

What are needs?

Really, is it something that has been predetermined for us to constantly spend our money on? What would life be like without having needs? Can you do without the things you say are needs?

Having a home is the place where you and your family can dwell privately. There are two ways to enjoy a home, one is home owner-ship, and another is renting.

If I could, I would make all of you home owners not renters. Being a homeowner is possibly the largest investment you will make. Your residence is a need, as well as food to eat, lights, a bed, and etc. Just think of the things that make a house a home.

We need clothes, regardless of our profession. There are standard needs for clothing. What environment would you feel comfortable in without good personal care? Depending on where you live, a car is your only means of transportation. These are some of the basic living expenses that are needed. There are some other needs that are demanded, unlike the basic living needs. Your job may require a suit and tie or business dress everyday. Needs are the products and serv-ices that we cannot live without.

What are wants?

If you have a reliable used car regardless if it is 2 years old or 7 years old, you want a new car. Wants are generally things you do not need. This area is such a challenge, because you can employ your creative imagination and justify a want into a need. Remember the three P's(provide, protect, and preserve), preserving the essence of a way of life, can help you deal with wants.

You know, we talked about the various styles of managing money earlier. Where or what styles would "wants" fit in. Items that make life a bit comfortable, or lifestyles more glamorous, are primarily "wants."

Regardless, distinguishing between needs and wants truly depends on the financial values or the lack of. Establishing financial values provides the manner in which a person will handle their money. Value is a key ingredient here and you can only set it for yourself.

Provide, Protect, and Preserve is the recipe for you to maintain or develop wealth. This is so personal that once you begin to undertake this task, you will have control over your money. Consider a person who values being a homeowner, they will have goals that will allow them to make it a priority. This priority will have the values to provide, protect, and preserve their continuous plight to remain a homeowner. They value ownership more than renting. The same is true with education, health, wealth, and many other things.

There is a unique way in which all of this begins to come together in a simple format. We have to break it up into small pieces to allow you the opportunity to do the same. Examine your own style of money management. Understand how your behavior impacts your spending, and the affects is has on you're saving. Know what your financial condition is by developing financial statements, balance sheets, and financial ratios. This way you are able to make a good assessment.

Distinguishing the differences between wants and needs allows your own values to take control. Trusting your own values system is far better for you than for you to choose mine. Remember the style "The Jones" is a person who requires and even demands the same products as friends, family, and neighbors. Many times these products normally cost more than what they can afford. They pattern their lifestyles after others, their clothes, household items, car, and homes.

LIABILITY?

This is an area that I found to be far more frightening than all that we have discussed already. The area of liability will have to be considered as well. Even though we spoke about it earlier we did not go in to any details.

Liabilities can have a direct affect on your future goals and decisions regarding your desire to build wealth. The homeowner we spoke of earlier has the liability of this debt. Let's say the cost of their home is $135,000, they paid $13,500.00 as a down payment. This homeowner will have the liability of $121,500.00 not including any interest paid over the life of the mortgage.

This is one of the good form of liability to have if you must have one and you must. The reason that I believe this to be a good liability is because the value of the home can increase, which will add value to your total net worth. Also, you can add value to the home that will help reduce the overall liability.

Your car is a liability as well, but it works a little differently than a home. Your car value will depreciate and your liability will basically remain the same. Each year a car loses a percentage of its value. It is very unlikely that a domestic car value will increase. Please under-stand that your home can also lose value as well but it's not likely in today's climate.

Before you answer the following questions, give some thought of you own liabilities. What are they?

Can you name just four of your major liabilities?

_____

_____

_____

_____

Out of the four that you have selected, which is the best to have? And in what order?

_____

_____

_____

We also have credit card debt, because many of us refuse to pay off the balance every month. Or we are so content to just pay the minimum requirement each month, that they become a very large liability. Consider this, if you carried a $5,000.00 balance on a 16% credit card and only paid the minimum requirement each month, with no new charges it will cost over $13,000.00 in interest. If that dose not scare you, it will take you nearly 46 years to pay it off. Now, I believe that is what you can call a liability.

Student Loans are also a liability that can cost you thousands of dollars over the life of repayment of the loan. There are other forms of liability as well. By now you should have come up with some idea of your own liabilities. Earlier we talked about what a balance sheet is, and mentioned how liabilities apply. To just refresh your memory, a balance sheet provides your net worth, by taking all of your liabilities from your assets. Assets are the total value to the things you own. **Liabilities are just the opposite, they are things you owe.**

Here is a list of Liabilities

- Current liabilities - debts you will pay off three to five years.
- Charge accounts, credit cards or other bills
- Installment credit / short term loans
- Unusual tax liabilities
- Long-term liabilities - future debt.
- Mortgage notes on personal real estate
- Mortgage notes on investment real estate
- Bank & Margin loans
- Life insurance loans

ASSETS

Assets are the total value of the things you own, and I do mean everything you own. When some one asks you what your net worth is, will you know the answer? Let's try something right now, take a moment and ask yourself what is your net worth? $.00 +/-. Write down what you think it is. After you have given it your best try, look at the items below to determine your assets. Then look at your liabilities and come up with that total. Now subtract the liabilities from the assets and you will have your net worth. What is your true net worth $_____.00 +/- after you have done the math.

You want to build wealth or become wealthy, but you won't without a list of items below. These items are wealth products. Each one is needed to build wealth. Some of them you will hear a lot about as you continue on this journey. Our focus will be on foundational products that offer some minimum risk to you.   Here is a list of assets.

Liquid assets - ready cash
Cash and checking acct.(s)
Savings account(s)
Money market funds
Life Ins. cash values
U. S. savings bonds
Brokerage accounts

Investment-long-term goals
Business interests
Investment real estate
Pension accounts
Tax - sheltered investments
Personal real estate
Vacation home/timeshare

Marketable investments
Common stocks
Mutual funds
Corporate bonds
Municipal bonds
Certificates of Deposit
IRA/other retirement plans
Profit-sharing accounts
Thrift plan accounts

Other assets/hobbies
Auto(s)
Boat(s)
Furs and jewelry
Collections, hobbies, etc.
Furniture/household items.
Other personal property

Determine financial goals (short and long term) and your assets and liabilities will play a great role as you establish a budget. All of this is geared towards helping you understand your financial condition. It's important that you consider all of the information you have read so far. All budgets must have goals in mind. Whether it's short term or long term, working with your own financial condition will determine your goals.

Let me also remind you that setting a budget is a family affair, but yet private. There are never two budgets that are the same. Let me say it this way, you cannot set a budget the way your best friend did. This may seem to be going in an area that you may feel does not apply to you, well, how can you not consider your condition before you set your goals.

What are some of your fears in setting or having a budget?
1. _____
2. _____
3. _____
4. _____

What are some of the reason couples divorce over money?

_____

_____

_____

_____

Give serious consideration to your current condition. Now what is it that you want?

_____

_____

You must set values as you begin to budget. Your budget is the first section to build wealth. Each piece of that section is very important, values, wants vs. needs, expenses, and styles are all needed for a successful budget.

CHAPTER THREE

PLANNING A BUDGET

Now, we can look at making a budget work for you. If you are single or have only one income in your household this budget will still work for you. Focusing on couples in setting up this budget plan provides relief to family problems. Money issues have been rated as the number one cause of divorce for years.

There have been many different books and comments on the reason that couples fight over money or the lack of money. Pastors have counseled families on the biblical principal of dealing with finances, yet the problems still exist. Different debt management programs have had very little impact. The question is why?

The reason that money issues are still a problem in most households is because neither partner understands how to manage money. That's right, we sometime find it difficult to except the fact that we are not able to manage our own money. It can be very humiliating admitting that we are not able to control our spending. A woman that is able to create reasons why she was at the mall spending, rather than paying the light bill, has the ability to create a budget. Men will stand their grounds on being the man, yet money mismanagement weakens their ability to boast.

Remember, we talked about spending styles earlier and the impact they have on your budget. There are other areas that have a direct affect on budgeting. They are; **self-awareness, conscience, creative imagination, and independent will.**

Self-awareness is the point and time that we know we need to do something, it's when we know what, when and how. Yet we convert our self-awareness into selfishness. Selfishness in deciding that this is what I want, right or wrong.

Conscience, the internal guidance system, which allows us to sense when we act or even, contemplates acting. We recognize the distinction between right and wrong, in regard to one's own conduct. Or, conforming to our own sense of right conduct.

Creative imagination is the point and time that we are able to justify the things we do or not do. Take Christmas time, we will put things off like the light bill, telephone, cable, or some other bills to buy gifts. We will go deeper in debt, knowing that our financial situation cannot handle any more debt.

Independent will allows us to really feel good about the decisions we make regardless of the outcome. It's the ability to act freely without any outside influences. The point in which we stand our ground on all of our decisions.

These areas can be used to your advantage as well, it will take independent will to be determined to reach your goals. With your creativeness you can develop methods that work for your home. Budgeting, when done properly, will provide you the freedom that you deserve. As we move forward with setting your budget, take into consideration your style, where you are, and your goals.

Okay, lets get started with setting up your budget. Before you do anything ask yourself. "Why am I doing this?" Your answer will set your pace. But for now, consider where you are, write down what you are currently doing with your money. I want you to really be honest with yourself. Look at your checkbook to see what items you paid in the last thirty days. Consider the information from the financial data sheet on page 18. This can serve as a chart to begin with.

Once you have written down all spending, get a total of all of the spending. Now, you look at you paycheck stub to determine your net income. That is your income after taxes, some of you may have loans with your employer or its credit union that takes a deduction before you receive your check. If this is the case, take this amount off of your budget sheet.

Example: You purchase your car though the company's credit union and they take out $150.00 each pay period after taxes, before you receive your check. This mean that your car payment will not show up on your budget.

Now, take a look at budget #1 on the next page, this should be similar to yours. Notice that we show the items that come out of the paycheck before we receive it. If you notice, there are three areas you need to look at. The amount that is being paid on one of the credit card debts, life style, and the remaining income. We will deal with the credit card debt later. This is a very large monthly payment for a credit card. For many households it is normal to have such a payment. With the remaining income we must begin to save money.

The items with the asterisk (*) symbols show your life styles, the thing that make you who you are. It also identifies the number one area of your budget. This area must be controlled and never compromised at anytime. If you compromise any of these areas to any degree, all of your goals can go up in smoke. This will be the first level of your financial foundation. Keep this in mine also, if you pay your mortgage on time you are able to borrow money at low rates. On the other hand if you do not pay on time, it is very hard to borrow money at all.

Let's look closely at what is going on here. Your household expenses are completely covered, it includes everything that makes you comfortable. Remember, provide, protect, and preserve is what a budget does for you. It will give you the balance that will allow you the opportunity to reach your goals.

Understanding what a budget is allows us to feel good about life. I remember the time when I was unable to pay my bills, going to work was hard. I needed to be there to earn money, while knowing that it was not enough. Now, we are going to divide this budget into three parts, household, personal, and debts. The total budget of expenses is $2,170.00, but only $1,102.00 is household expenses. Household expense provides the way for you to preserve your lifestyle. Can you imagine no lights, water, cable or telephone in your home?

Personal expenses are food, personal care, gasoline, and household expenses. These expenses total $340.00, giving you the pleasure to enjoy your labor. This is money that you spend on you and your family. Before you say that is not a lot of money, remember this is what we identified.

Depending on styles, you are able to really be who you are. The way you look, dress, and act is all wrapped up in the personal expenses. For many there are no entertainment, no activities outside of the home. Now, there must be something else here that is going on that we are not seeing. Just $340.00 is not enough for personal expenses, some lifestyle. Right!!!

Well, in addition to $340.00 there is $330.00 that is left as remaining income that can go towards your personal care or your debts. Now, your personal expenses total can almost double with this additional money. As you will see with the next budget we made some changes. This is where self-awareness, conscience, creative imagination, and independent will really kick in. What you do, how you do it, and just simply what goals you set makes a budget work.

Finally, the debt total is a whopping $728.00, 29% of your total net income. Over $8,700.00 a year in credit card debt, this money is going someone else. Look at it this way, $3,319.00 is applied to your credit card debt and $5,416.00 goes to your creditors wow. This is one areas that we must reduce if we are going to be able to build wealth. Would you agree? We will deal with this with more clarity to eliminate this trend.

BUDGET # 1

*Rent/ Mortgage	$700.00	*Home/Renters Ins.	$ -----
*Sewer	$20.00	*Club Fees	$0.00
*Water	$20.00	*Entertainment	$0.00
*Lights	$92.00	*Household	$40.00
*Gas	$54.00	*Saving	$0.00
*Cable	$0.00	**Credit Cards/Other Debts**	
*Telephone	$40.00		
*Food Expenses	$175.00	MNA	$49.00
*Child Care	$ -----	Victoria Secrets	$15.00
*Clothing Expenses	$ -----	1st Visa	$100.00
*Health	$ Paycheck	**MBA**	**$315.00**
*Life	$ Paycheck	Rich's	$39.00
*Auto	$101.00	Beneficial	$85.00
*Car Payment	$ Paycheck	Phoenix Fed C/U	$125.00
*Taxes	$75.00		
*Church Tithes	$0.00	**Total Income**	**$2500.00**
*Personal Care	$50.00	**Total Debt**	**$2170.00**
*Gasoline Expenses	$75.00		
*Alimony/Support	$0.00	**Remaining**	**$330.00**

We took the same budget and made some helpful changes, changes we believe will provide greater freedom. Budget #2, here we try to make this more affordable to you. The first change we made was to give money in the area of tithes and offering. This is done according to your own faith.

Let me also say that your creditors do not believe as you do about tithes and offering. They will tell you to pay your bills, and stop giving money to that man. Well, according to your obedience to the Word of God you must tithe. If you have to show a creditor your budget remember he will not understand tithing.

We also reduced that large payment to the MBNA account as well, the minimum is only $75.00. Paying that extra $240.00 was not making an impact. (This we will talk about a little later.) We added money to entertainment, clothes, and savings. Entertainment, clothes, is very important to place in your budget. This helps the family to preserve their way of life. Your tithes and savings go directly to household expenses, while you include entertainment, and clothes to personal expenses.

Now, let's look at these numbers and compare to see if there is an advantage over budget #1. It is very important that you understand the changes that we have made. As you will see later, the advantages can be extremely great if done properly.

I would like for you to track how we dealt with the expenses. So, we are going to continue to use this same budget all the way though this book. The total expenses are $2,395.00, and the household expenses jump to $1,302.00. The personal expenses total are now $565.00, with $105.00 remaining. The debt dropped to $528.00, 21% of net income. On the next page, study the difference carefully. You may have to make similar changes in your budget.

BUDGET # 2		*Telephone	$40.00
*Rent/Mortgage	$700.00	*Food Expenses	$175.00
*Sewer	$20.00	*Child Care	$ -----
*Water	$20.00	*Clothing Expense	$75.00
*Lights	$92.00	Health	$ Paycheck
*Gas	$54.00	Life	$ Paycheck
*Cable	$0.00	*Auto	$101.00

Car Payment	$ Paycheck
* Taxes	$75.00
*Church Tithes	$100.00
*Personal Care	$50.00
*Gasoline Expenses	$75.00
*Alimony/Support	$0.00
Home/Renters Ins.	$ -----
*Club Fees	$0.00
*Entertainment	$150.00
*Household	$40.00
*Saving	$100.00

Credit Cards/Other Debts

MBA	$49.00
Victoria Secrets	$15.00
1st Visa	$100.00
MBA	$75.00 + $40.00
Rich's	$39.00
Beneficial	$85.00
Phoenix Fed C/U	$125.00
Total Income	**$2500.00**
Total Debt	**$2395.00**
Remaining	**$105.00**

You are probably asking yourself a few questions by now, I hope that we guess right. How does the two budgets differ? What are your advantages? What bills do you pay first? Let me answer these question this way. Budget #2 provides a more effective plan because it allows saving, and all of your personal cares can be met.

Dealing with the debt, by paying an additional $240.00 as in budget #1 really is not making that great of a difference. You can receive nearly the same affect by spending only $40.00 separate from the minimum payment.

Looking at budget #3 you will notice that there are items with ** symbol, these bills are paid on the 1st or 5th of the month. With the items that are in the shaded area divide them in half to balance your money and activities evenly. Now, for the shaded area you will repeat it on the 15th or 20th of the month, and add the remaining debt also. This reduces the time you spend trying to figure out what to pay first.

The system will allow you the opportunity to reduce stress between you and your mate. The numbers are now set, all you have to do is make the deposit and write the checks. This will consume about one hour a month of your precious time.

Now, you can begin to save and build the first level of your journey to creating wealth. What you do with the savings will be covered later. The goal here will be to just get started. Once you are confident in your budget and have put some money in a saving account, you should be very proud.

Someone had said to me once after going over budget #3, that $100.00 a month is not a lot of money. They even turned their nose up at me when I said that was $1,200.00 a year. So, I asked them when was the last time you had $1,200.00 in a saving account? I mean money that you have saved, not your 401k or money from a tax refund, gift or any form whereby you did not save it. And now, I'm asking you, when was the last time you had just $1,000.00 saved?

This example is to give you a simple approach, if you have more discretionary income you are able to save more. For single income individuals just putting away $20.00 a week is $1040.00 a year. Even if you believe that you are living paycheck to pay check, you waste at least $20 a week.

This is about changing your concept of dealing with money and your values. Not that you should believe in my value system, you should have your own. It seem that we continue to refer back to the area of styles. Styles are the comfort zone the we are in. Our goals are formed directly or indirectly based on the style we use. Consider a person that uses check-cashing facilities weekly, giving 3% to 6% of his or her paycheck as a fee.

If this persons' check is $400.00 a week, that is $12 to $26 wasted weekly. It's wasted only when that person does not understand that there are other ways to cash checks. Their fear may be the cost of having a checking account, not realizing that most banks will not charge a fee if you maintain an average balance. That $26 a week can work towards building that minimum amount to offset the cost.

On the other hand, this is a style, it is mismanagement, and in principal not much different than the way most people mishandle money. As we move forward, we will deal with saving money a lot more. The idea of budgeting is to have a plan, a plan that allows you to control your money. Budgeting is the staging area or the foundation of building wealth. To many, it's about the many investment products that you may have. What happens when those products are not there?

BUDGET #3

**Rent/Mortgage	$700.00	*Club Fees	$0.00
*Sewer	$ 20.00	*Entertainment	$150.00
*Water	$20.00	*Household	$40.00
*Lights	$92.00	*Saving	$100.00
*Gas	$54.00	**Credit Cards/Other Debts**	
*Cable	$0.00		
*Telephone	$40.00	MBA	$49.00
*Food Expenses	$175.00	Victoria Secrets	$15.00
*Child Care	$ -----	1st Visa	$100.00
*Clothing Expenses	$75.00	MBA	$75.00 + $40.00
Health	$Paycheck	Rich's	$39.00
Life	$Paycheck	Beneficial	$85.00
**Auto	$101.00	Phoenix Fed C/U	$125.00
Car Payment	$Paycheck		
*Personal Taxes	$75.00		
**Church Tithes	$100.00	**Total Income**	**$2500.00**
*Personal Care	$50.00	**Total Debt**	**$2395.00**
*Gasoline Expenses	$75.00		
*Alimony/Support	$0.00	**Remaining**	**$105.00**
Home/Renters Ins.	$-----		

Without a budget how can you possibly know how money it takes for you to have financial freedom.

CHAPTER FOUR

ARE YOU IN FINANCIAL TROUBLE?

Damage, Just How Much?

It is important that you are fully aware of how much debt you are actually carrying no matter how painful it is. Earlier, we asked you to identify your liabilities-now we are changing liabilities to the dirty word **DEBT.** You must familiarize yourself with the amounts of all your debts, as the names of family members. Knowing the total of them, the amount of interest that is charged, the grace periods and everything else about your debt. Keep the amounts and the information fixed in your mind.

They say that pain and pleasure are powerful motivators in people lives. If this is true, carrying the pain of your debt with you is heavy enough, you will want to take aggressive measures to lighten your load. There is a simple way to deal with debt. Before we begin to eliminate your debts, let's look at some facts and myths regarding credit and debt.

This is the area that causes more people like yourself to just give up. When you begin to realize that you may have a financial problem, it's easy to deny it. The burden of debt, will cause you to loose sleep, not answer your telephone at home, afraid to get your mail, and create stress in your home. Overextended debt will ruin your marriage.

Now, we must examine and understand how credit card debt, installment loans, and lines of credit really affect your financial life. Is credit card debt wrong for you? No. How you deal with credit card debt, as well as any other debt, is the determining factor.

Let's talk about the things (debts) that can get you in trouble. Just as we talked about the process of creating a budget, we'll look at the different types of debt. As we look at the types of debt, it will be important to also evaluate the condition of the credit that is extended. All types of credit are not created equal, therefore the more you understand it, and the better you can deal with it.

There are essentially four types of consumer credit:

• Mortgage Loans.

We have talked a little about mortgage loans, remember it could possibly represent the largest financial transaction you will make. Mortgages typically are amortized over 15, 20, 25 or even 30 years. There are many types of mortgages available and many of them offer different repayment and interest options. Amortization covers many years, and the total amount of interest could be considerable.

• Personal Term Loans/Installment Loans

Personal term loans are for a fixed amount of money, called the principal, and are repaid over a set term or simple interest. The total cost of the loan is the principal plus the interest. Different lending institutions offer different features with their personal loans, including flexible repayment options and variable interest rates.

• Personal Lines Of Credit

Lines of credit are very similar to a business line of credit: You arrange for an amount of money to be available to you on demand.

You "draw down" on your line of credit by writing a check. You are charged interest only for the amount of money you have drawn down. A line of credit are like writing yourself a loan whenever you need it.

• Credit Cards

Credit cards are revolving credit, which means that the amount of credit varies with your purchases and cash advances, versus the payments you make to reduce your balance. Credit cards typically carry higher interest rate compared to other forms of credit. Many believe that they offer a greater convenience and other features that in some circumstances tend to offset the higher interest rates charged. "Wrong"

Unsecured debt, such as credit cards, carries high interest rates that reflect the unsecured nature of the loan. The little plastic cards that most people carry in their wallets are in three basic categories:

Traditional Credit Cards

These let you borrow up to a pre-set limit and pay it back at your own pace, as long as you make the monthly minimum payment. You will pay interest on any outstanding balance that you carry on your account month-to-month. The interest rate charged can vary substantially from card to card, and is among the most important criteria for choosing the right card. Larger chain stores also issue charge cards, acceptable only at their own stores. Again, be sure you fully understand all interest rate and payment terms before entering into an agreement to use any of these cards.

Debit Cards/Check Cards

Though they resemble credit cards, debit cards really work like checks. The money you spend is immediately deducted from a bank or brokerage account, and you therefore pay no interest on the money you spend. ATM, (automated teller machine), cards are the most common example of debit cards, and many are now accepted at stores for purchases. Depending on your personal credit situation, using debit cards may be a good strategy for avoiding credit card interest.

Travel & Entertainment cards

Like traditional credit cards, T&E cards are used to make purchases, and the issuer extends credit to you. However, the issuer expects you to pay the bill in full each month, rather than finance it at your pace. As a result, T&E cards do not charge you interest—instead, they make their money by charging merchants a percentage of each sale executed with the card.

RETROACTIVE INTEREST RATE HIKES

If you sign up for a credit card with a low "teaser" rate, such as 4.9%, when the low rate period expires, your existing balance will likely be subject to the regular and substantially higher interest rate. In most cases, it can go as high as 23.9%, if you do not pay it in full before the rate period expires. Another concern about interest rate is how most card issuers charge interest from the very first day your charge is posted. Also, some charge interest from the date of your purchase. It always good to pay in full monthly to avoid interest charges.

DUE DATES & FEES

Card issuers offer a 25-day grace period in which to pay for new purchases without incurring finance charges. Some have even cut your grace period to 20 days or less. This normally affects only the customers who pay in full. You could pay up to $50 a year or more on annual fee for each credit card. You may also be subject to finance charges of over 18%. There are offers with great credit limits, and lots of features with "strings" attached. Strings such as no grace period. Remember they charge interest on everything from the day you buy it.

By carrying a balance from month to month, there is no grace period on new purchases with most cards. Your grace period may not apply if you don't pay in full monthly. Almost all credit cards impose both finance charges and a transaction fee on cash advances.

Interest starts from the day of the advance, and the transaction fee can be up to 2.5% of the cash advance withdrawn. Transferring a balance is also a cash advance. Transaction fees may still apply, even if they say no finance charges.

Charge cards, include travel and entertainment cards, such as American Express or Diner's club and most gasoline cards. Credit cards include: some department store cards and MasterCard, Visa, and Discover cards. Generally, charge cards must be paid in full each month, while credit cards can be paid over time.

As you can see there are many different elements that you should consider when using credit. Credit used wisely, is a useful tool that can help you extend a payment schedule, for emergencies or major purchases. Always remember that there is a cost associated with using credit. Never use credit to extend your budget beyond your ability to meet obligations.

Keep this in mind, just because no payment is due until January '2010, it's not always the best. There are credit companies that offer sales of merchandise with no payment for many months even up to a year. Can you imagine buying a sofa that family and friends has just flopped down on time and time again until it's broken. A sofa that you no longer have need of, and now the first payment is due.

Okay, so you bought it with no interest, and no down payment. The end result is that now you have to buy a new one and pay for it also. Credit can cost. Do not be fooled. You've heard the phrase "pay me now or pay me later." **It's a cost you will pay.**

HOW MUCH IS ENOUGH?

How much does credit really cost you? Is the cost of credit too much for you to bear? When I think of the amount of consumer debt today, and the new levels that it has reached. I am amazed that while consumer spending has climbed, the level of savings a dropped. Even some economists are optimistic about how high the debt level is today. There are some that feel that there are many signs that the amount of consumer debt is slowing which is an improvement. But, with the deceptive tactics the banks and credit card companies are using, there is no improvement.

- Billions of unsolicited mail
- Deceptive card rate offers
- Late payment tricks
- Outrageous fees and penalties

Once you use these credit cards, some of the things that they will hit you with should be illegal.

- $25 annual penalty fee on consumers who pay on time
- Late one time there is a penalty
- Two times, your interest rate skyrockets as high as 23%
- They even help make your payment late.
- Up to $30 penalty if you are late one day
- One to three days grace period with only a third of the banks, other - no more grace periods

Low "teaser" rate, such as 4.9% -- then it jumps as high 23.9%. If your rate goes from 15% to 23% on an average $5,000.00, it will boost your total interest cost by $4,000.00 over the next 10 years.

Interest Rates

Interest rates are the number one burden that consumers face in dealing with debt. Often times, the amount of interest is not an issue with consumers when that independent will steps in and say "I want it." Everything from gas in your car, to your mortgage, require interest to be paid. We never consider the fact that when you spend $40.00 on gas a month and make the minimum payment it can us cost $100.00 for that amount of gas. Interest rates come in different forms. Depending on the type that is used, it can cost you.

Here are eight type of interest rates that you will encounter at some point.

Rule of 72 - The estimation of doubling time on an investment, for which the compounded annual rate of return times the number of years must equal roughly 72 for the investment to double in value.

Rule of 78 - A formula used to determine rebates on interest for installment loans; since $1 + 2 + ... + 12 = 78$, 1/78th of the interest is owed after the first month, 3/78ths after the second month, etc.

Prime Rate - The interest rate that commercial banks charge their most creditworthy borrowers, such as large corporations. The prime rate is a lagging indicator, also called prime.

Interest Rate - Interest per year divided by principal amount, expressed as a percentage.

Adjustable Rate - An interest rate, which can be periodically adjusted up or down, usually in response to, changes in the prime rate. Also called variable rate or floating rate, opposite of fixed rate.

Fixed-Rate - A loan in which the interest rate does not change during the entire term of the loan, opposite of adjustable rate.

Simple Interest - The interest calculated on a principal sum, not compounded on earned interest.

Annual Percentage Rate (APR) - The yearly cost of a mortgage, including interest, mortgage insurance, and the origination fee (points), expressed as a percentage.

Trying to understand the cost of interest to a loan can be very hard. On credit cards it depends on the (APR) Annual Percentage Rates and the length of your loan. With a balance of $5000.00 and a interest rate of 21% your interest for one month is $87.50. How did I come up this number? It's really simple. Multiply your balance by the (APR) 21% and divide it by 12. Over the course of one year with and average balance of $5000.00 your interest paid will be $1050.00. Now, with this example, you only paid the 2% minimum each month, only $12.50 will reduce the principle balance. Your projection to pay this debt off would be over 500 months. This is longer than the time it would take you to pay off a $100,000.00 mortgage. **Credit can really cost you.**

THE MYTHS

Changing your behavior is key to attacking debt. I'm sure that you have read many books on debt relief, but yet, you still find yourself in financial trouble. Many financial consultants suggest that consumers begin to deny themselves to attack debt. Other says a sacrifice of some personal items will allow you to eliminate your debts. I just think about the number of people who quit their diets because the sacrifice was too much for them.

Tearing up your credit cards, literally taking a pair of scissors and cutting them up may not be enough. Calling your credit card company and telling them to close your accounts is not enough. You might keep one card with a low limit set by you, not the credit card company. Applying for a low interest rate credit card and transferring your balances, can be disastrous.

Some recommend that you pay off your highest interest rate card first. Paying a little more than the minimum may shave months off your debt.

On your other debts, continue to pay just the minimum. After you finish paying off the highest interest rate cards, move on to the next highest interest rate. This will only be effective if you do it the right way, we will talk more about debt reduction later.

Don't get lured into those introductory, low-interest rate cards, which are so popular right now. Read the fine print before you apply. What they don't tell you is that the balance, which is transferred, is now a cash advance. This cash advance has a temporary interest rate that will jump back up to a high interest rate after 4 to 6 months. You're back to where you started or even worse! If you have used a low, introductory rate, have a plan to pay off the transferred balance within the allotted time. If not, you could very well be caught off guard.

You Can Be Sued

If you don't pay a debt, the most likely consequence is that you will be sued, unless the creditor thinks you are judgment proof. Being judgment proof means that you don't have any money or property that can legally be taken to pay the debt and aren't likely to get any soon. But because most court judgments last many years (up to 20 years in some states), and can often be renewed indefinitely, people who are broke may nevertheless be sued on the creditor's assumption that someday they'll come into money or property.

Similarly, very old people or people with terminal illness who are judgment proof may get sued by their creditors simply because the creditors know that it's easier to collect the debt at death (through the probate process) if they have a judgment than if they don't. Being judgment proof doesn't mean that you have no money or property at all, although many people who are judgment proof have virtually nothing. Being judgment proof means that if a creditor obtains a court judgment, you are allowed to keep all of your property.

Each state has declared certain items of property beyond the reach of creditors--these items are called exempt property. Suffice to say that if you are receiving no income except government benefits, such as Social Security or unemployment, and have limited personal property and no real property, you are judgment proof, at least right now.

If a creditor sues you in regular court (as opposed to small claims court) you can fight the lawsuit. If you don't oppose the lawsuit, or you let the court automatically enter a judgment against you (called a default judgment), however, the case could be over in 30 to 60 days.

If the creditor gets a judgment, he has a number of ways to enforce it. If you are working, the most common method is to attach your wages, meaning that up to 25% of your take-home pay is removed from your paycheck and sent to the creditor before you ever see it.

The next most common method to collect a judgment is to seize your deposit accounts. They can actually have your bank seize every dime you may have in the bank. Up to the amount of money that you owe on the judgment. In chapter 11, we show you the federal regulations regarding wage attachments. Keep in mind that state law may differ in the amount that can be seized.

Later in this book we will show some of the letters we have used that have been very successful. Each situation can be dealt with to your advantage with the need to file bankruptcy. Bankruptcy can only complicate your life.

CHAPTER FIVE

DOING IT
FOR YOURSELF

Living an irresponsible carefree life, from paycheck to paycheck, really doesn't offer much when you begin looking at perhaps what the future might hold. In this part of the book we hope to motivate you to open up your mind to effectively change. As a consumer, you must take control of every area of your financial life. In taking control, you must plan each step as would an artist working on a masterpiece. First, gather all of the tools you will need: knowledge, wisdom and understanding. Once you have actually put each to use, you will then notice how you have empowered yourself to change your finances.

Knowledge can be gained through reading and listening. That which is learned and understood, gives you the ability to be aware of your situation. Knowing your situation and using the experiences you have gained will give you the wisdom. Wisdom will provide you with the insight to make better judgments, use common sense and to have total comprehension of all you need to be successful financially. We talked about the importance of foundation in Chapter One. The framework that is placed on the foundation will be the knowledge you have gained already.

Understanding what you waste.
(daily, weekly, monthly, annually)

Realizing my own fears (limitations, what others think, I can't do it).

Locating the information needed.

Checking my attitude (resentment, dwelling on the past, uncaring).

Because credit is personal and most of us feel that we may have failed by making unwise choices, it's encouraging to know that someone else has overcome some of the same problems you face!! It could be that coworker who seems to have it all going for himself or the neighbor that just recently bought that new home. This is not just a problem that was designed or tailor made just for you. Statistics show that three out of five households experience financial difficulty at some point.

AIR WAVE

With wisdom, what can you use to make the changes and take away the fears that have developed over time? I have started using a plan that I truly think is responsible for some of the changes that helped me turn my financial life around. The A-I-R-W-A-V-E plan is simple, but complicated in that you have to work at it everyday.

A - Action (You bought the workbook.)

I - Information (I'm providing the information.)

R - Reading (You must complete this workbook.)

W - Waste less (Put a value on your time.)

Attitude - (If you want something you never had, do something you've never done.)

V - Vision (I cannot visualize this for you, only you can.)

E - Empowerment (Now, what are you going to do about it?)

The "A" must be put to work daily. It requires a specific action on your part. The "I" has to work together with the "R." Information that is obtained by reading will provide you direction. The "W" is used as a motivating tool to your goals and causes you to utilize all that you have without waste.

My "A" is my own attitude that I carry around everyday. It must be in control. Where would I be without "V," having the vision of what may lie ahead. Last, but not least, "E" is the empowerment that I may accomplish all of my dreams.

Use the "action" that came forth from the "information" that you have been "reading." Without "waste" of time or energy maintaining the "attitude" the you must never lose sight of the "vision." It is the vision of knowledge that gives understanding to the concepts that wisdom creates "self-empowerment" which is now within your own hands.

Write a clear, concise statement of what actions you need to take to reach your goals.

_____

_____

_____

_____

_____

_____

_____

_____

_____

Now set some reasonable goals to reach.

_____

_____

_____

_____

_____

_____

Some would have you to ask yourself questions like:

1. **Should we sell our home and buy or even rent a smaller place until we get back on our feet financially?**
2. **Should we move to a different area where housing is less expensive?**
3. **Do I really need to buy premium gas?**
4. **Why not wait and rent a movie, instead of paying $10-$12 to go to the theater?**
5. **Do I really need all those magazine subscriptions?**
6. **Do I really need those movie channels?**
7. **Could I live without cable TV?**
8. **Do I really use my bottled water service?**
9. **What are some cheaper alternatives?**
10. **Do I really need a new dress, suit, purse, and jewelry this month?**

How you answer these questions all depends on how quickly you want to get out of debt. But, I believe that you can get out of debt without penalizing yourself. The ten items above can make wanting to change difficult, but will cause you to take an honest assessment of yourself.

We hope to show you how to deal with debt by making changes. Also, to enlighten you on simple principles that will bring the same results.

Getting out of debt will not be easy without a plan. That plan must begin with a budget, then a savings account. As important as changing your money habits are, without a plan and complete understanding, you are just spinning your wheels.

Getting out of debt, is not paying off bills. Getting completely out is changing your overall financial attitude and portfolio. The purpose of being out of debt is to build wealth, and to provide security for our families. We want to reverse the cycle of how we have managed our money in the past. After learning your style, setting a budget, targeting our debt load, and setting a plan, it is finished.

How to Attack Your Debt & Manage Your Money

Lesson 1

Can't pay your bills? You're not alone. Today, millions of Americans are having difficulty paying their debts. Most of those in financial distress are middle-income families who want to pay off what they owe. Some individuals really never give thought concerning finances. When most people think about building wealth, they are thinking primarily about investing. Well, we are going to continue our process in investing in yourself. Using your ability to eliminate debt and create wealth. We will revisit budget 1 & 2, and totally understand how to get out of debt.

BUDGET # 1

*Rent	$700.00	*Alimony/Support	$0.00
*Sewer	$20.00	*Home/Renters Ins.	$-----
*Water	$20.00	*Club Fees	$0.00
*Lights	$92.00	*Entertainment	$0.00
*Gas	$54.00	*Household	$40.00
*Cable	$0.00	*Saving	$0.00
*Telephone	$40.00	**Credit Cards/Other Debts**	
*Food Expenses	$175.00	MNA	$49.00
*Child Care	$ -----	Victoria Secrets	$15.00
*Clothing Expenses	$	1st Visa	$100.00
*Health	$ Paycheck	MBA	$315.00
*Life	$ Paycheck	Rich's	$39.00
*Auto	$101.00	Beneficial	$85.00
*Car Payment	$ Paycheck	Phoenix Fed C/U	$125.00
*Taxes	$75.00	**Total Income**	**$2500.00**
*Church Tithes	$0.00	**Total Debt**	**$2170.00**
*Personal Care	$50.00	**Remaining**	**$330.00**
*Gasoline Expenses	$75.00		

Looking at budget #1 we have a family with the income of $2500.00 a month after a car payment, insurance and taxes.

For this budget, this family is renters, not home owners. They have a total of debt, including the car of $28,090.00.

MNA	$500.00	Rich's	$190.00
Victoria Secrets	$300.00	Beneficial	$1,300.00
1st Visa	$4,000.00	Phoenix Fed C/U	$1,800.00
MBA	$7,000.00	Car	$13,000.00

With this illustration it will be important that we show you the expected amount of time to pay this debt off. This way, you will be able to appreciate the result that we intend to show you.

MNA	18%	3 yrs.	Rich's	21%	2 yrs.
Victoria Secrets	18%	2 yrs.	Beneficial	15%	2 yrs.
1st Visa	16%	20 yrs.	Phoenix C/U	14%	1 yrs.
MBA	21%	35 +	Car	17%	4 yrs.

The average amount of time that this family will get out of debt is 8.81 years. This would mean that we will need to reduce the amount of time. Now, if this family filed your personal bankruptcy, let's say a Chapter 7, that would mean all of the unsecured debt will be eliminated. They still will have to make the car payment and any other secured debts payments. Not to mention that the bankruptcy would be on their credit file for 10 years.

What if they went to a debt management company or filed for a Chapter 13 instead? A debt management company will pay your bills for you each month, and that can take five years. The Chapter 13, which is very similar, would take about the same amount of time. So, what difference can you make yourself?

By using either of these methods, what would you really learn? So, you are out of debt, you have not really bettered yourself. Believe it or not, this is a process that has been in place for years.

How does this benefit you? Where is the advantage for you? How would we deal with this problem? What would be the time saved? I am so happy you asked.

This family has learned how to properly manage their money. They have set a budget to give them greater control, along with financial freedom. Realizing that they had to make budget changes, they moved quickly. First, let me point out that because they are renters, there are no tax advantages at all. I will repeat this: No tax advantages at all. Neither is there any form of savings. If you look at budget #2 you will see the changes that they made.

BUDGET # 2

*Rent/Mortgage	$700.00	*Gasoline Expenses	$75.00
*Sewer	$20.00	*Alimony/Support	$0.00
*Water	$20.00	Home/Renters Ins.	$ -----
*Lights	$92.00	*Club Fees	$0.00
*Gas	$54.00	*Entertainment	$100.00
*Cable	$0.00	*Household	$40.00
*Telephone	$40.00	*Saving	$100.00
*Food Expenses	$175.00	**Credit Cards/Other Debts**	
*Child Care	$ -----	MBA	$49.00
*Clothing Expenses	$75.00	Victoria Secrets	$15.00
Health	$ Paycheck	1st Visa	$48.00 + $52.00
Life	$ Paycheck	MBA	$25.00 + $40.00
*Auto	$101.00	Rich's	$39.00
Car Payment	$ Paycheck	Beneficial	$85.00
*Taxes	$75.00	Phoenix Fed C/U	$125.00
*Church Tithes	$100.00	**Total Income**	**$2500.00**
*Personal Care	$50.00	**Total Debt**	**$2395.00**
		Remaining	**$105.00**

The very first thing I would like for you to notice is that they are now contributing to the church, they set up a savings account, their entertainment was adjusted a little. The keys to their reduction are this, the Visa and Mba accounts. They are paying the minimum payment of $48.00 and a second payment of $52.00. This second payment reduces the amount of interest charged the following month. Why would it do that? They are changing the average daily balance. By doing this, it has a greater impact than sending both payments together.

In just an eight-month period they would have saved some $1200.00. This money would now be a part of what's used to pay off debt. They would pay off MNA, Victoria Secrets, and Rich's. These three accounts were an average of 2 years, resolve in eight months. It only took about $825.00, which leaves about $375.00 in savings. Notice the changes in the MBA account in budget #1 the payment amount is $315.00.

But, budget #2 shows a dramatic reduction in the payment. Would you believe that the second budget would have a much greater affect on the balance? We talked about the impact earlier. There is now and additional $ 103.00 back into the budget from paying off three of the others.

Now that we have this additional $ 103.00, plus that same system that is in place, we will target MBA. We will be able to pay off this debt in another 20 months. The total saving is already in the mid thousands of dollars. Okay, we're going to combine all of this together so you can see how it worked.

The car payment is fixed, and so is Beneficial, and the credit union. So far we are at less than 3 years. The credit union was paid off in 1 Ω years, beneficial in 2 years. Once the credit union is paid off, the payment to Visa doubled in the same manner. Two separate payments, one at $48.00 the other at $ 152.00, which pays off the Visa some 9 months later.

It took 28 months, 2 years and 4 months to eliminate over $15,000.00 in debt. But at the same time this family saved $3715.00 in a personal saving account. They have an additional $578.00 of income to increase the savings plan.

What was once forecasting at least and average of 8 years was accomplished in less than 2 years, while the family wealth increased at the same time. I know you want to see those number a little bit clearer. And if I don't show you the numbers, what would be the point of this book?

This is what happens to the family over the twenty-eight month period.

- They were saving a $100.00 in their long term saving account, it would have totaled $ 2800.00. While at the same time they were putting away in an emergency account $50.00, which totaled $ 1600.00

- During the eighth months you recalled they paid off three creditors. They used only a portion of that savings, which was $825.00 over the remaining period. That left a savings balance of $ 3575.00.

- After paying off the three accounts it freed up $103.00, they add this money to the MBA account second payment. Which took another twenty months to pay it off. That total pay ended up looking like this: $125.00 for the minimum and $143.00 as the additional payment.

- Then starting with the first month to the eighteenth they paid off the credit union.

- From the first month we had twenty-four months to pay off beneficial. Because there were four more months left, we took that $ 85.00 payment and save it also. That saving totaled $340.00. Added to the other savings we had $3715.00 in total.

• Taking $125.00 from the credit union payment after it was paid off paid off the Visa. That made it ten payments of $48.00 plus $152.00 over the next ten months. There you have it, you can do it also. I make it sound of simple, but the tough directive here is discipline and self control.

Now let me give you something else about this family. Even though we got almost completely out of debt, there is a problem. It's not the car payment, with the return of $578.00 they could double up on the car payment.

The problem is this, if they were homeowners they could have had a tax write off. Being a renter the tax break goes to the landlord, that means they lost over $ 17,000.00 to the landlord. WOW

Lesson 2

Our purpose is to develop wealth-building skills to establish financial independence. In order for us to really convey this message properly, I feel the need to show these type of examples.

In the next story we will show how a homeowner was able to work out of the same situation. This example will show some of the advantages that the homeowner can use. People have always used equity in their home to do a variety of things. For most of them everything went well, but, for many they fell into a deeper hole.

Remember, when you are working out a financial problem, you must remember protecting your family, your home, and your character. In the next chapter you will see why your character is so important. I'm sure you understand why your family and home are priorities.

Provide, protect, and preserve is what I hope you are learning as we get out of debt. This next family will operate with the same obligation as the first family. I believe that you will be impressed by the results more then the solution. Let me remind you to think about all that you have read so far, and demand that you reread chapter 1 & 2.

That will help you focus on the primary reason we are doing things this way. Also, it may hit home with you again just in case you're not sure how to apply this information. Now, if you are skipping around in the book you may have missed something. Using your ability to eliminate debt and create wealth. We will revisit the same budgets 1 & 2, I want you to really understand how they got out of this debt.

BUDGET # 1

*Rent	$700.00	*Gasoline Expenses	$75.00
*Sewer	$20.00	*Alimony/Support	$0.00
*Water	$20.00	*Home/Renters Ins.	$ -----
*Lights	$92.00	*Club Fees	$0.00
*Gas	$54.00	*Entertainment	$ 0.00
*Cable	$0.00	*Household	$40.00
*Telephone	$40.00	*Saving	$0.00
*Food Expenses	$175.00	**Credit Cards/Other Debts**	
*Child Care	$ -----		
*Clothing Expenses	$	MNA	$49.00
*Health	$ Paycheck	Victoria Secrets	$15.00
*Life	$ Paycheck	1st Visa	$100.00
*Auto	$101.00	**MBA**	**$ 315.00**
*Car Payment	$ Paycheck	Rich's	$39.00
*Taxes	$75.00	Beneficial	$85.00
*Church Tithes	$0.00	Phoenix Fed C/U	$125.00
*Personal Care	$50.00	**Total Income**	**$2500.00**
		Total Debt	**$2170.00**
		Remaining	**$330.00**

Looking at Budget #1 this family income is also $2500.00 a month after a car payment, insurance and taxes. This homeowners they have a total of debt, including the car of $28,090.00.

MNA	$500.00	Rich's	$190.00
Victoria Secrets	$300.00	Beneficial	$1,300.00
1st Visa	$4,000.00	Phoenix Fed C/U	$1,800.00
MBA	$7,000.00	Car	$13,000.00

We have already discussed this amount of debt and the expected amount of time to pay this debt off.

MBA	18%	3 yrs.	Rich's	21%	2 yrs
Victoria Secrets	18%	2 yrs.	Beneficial	15%	2 yrs.
1st Visa	16%	20 yrs.	Phoenix Fed	4%	1 yrs.
MBA	21%	35 +	Car	17%	4 yrs.

The average amount of time for lesson 1 and that family to get out of debt was 8.81 years. That meant that they had to reduce the amount of time. We also talked about what filing personal bankruptcy, would do for them. We mention going to a debt management company or file for a Chapter 13 it could take five years. Looking at other solutions, we saw that by using either of the above methods, what they learned. Where would they have an advantage?

This family has learned to properly manage their money and set a budget that gave them greater control, along with financial freedom. Realizing that they had to make some budget changes they moved much quicker. Being homeowners, they wanted to have a tax advantages. They wanted a greater savings capacity than they currently had. If you look at Budget #2 you will see the changes they made.

They had equity in their property to borrow against that allowed them to do what many people have fail to do when they first looked for something in this area. This budget is far greater than what we discussed in lesson 1.

As you will see, they have really changed their direction completely. When you look at the changes that were made, you may wonder what really happened with this family. Well, it was not as simple as it looked, there are a number of major concerns they had before they made any decision with what you see in Budget #2.

A debt consolidation loan creates concerns with whether or not this will be a second mortgage, what will be the interest rate, what type of terms, and if there is An early pay off penalty. For you, this is not that simple. Each of those concerns can cost them a lot of money. It could also have cost them their home. There is a right and wrong way to use equity or a debt consolidation loan.

Taking a look at the concerns and risk, a second mortgage could have worked for them. But, that would have been a second lien on the property. Most second mortgages carry a very high interest rate. Not only is it at a higher interest, it also has a pre payment penalty. As we look closely at the results you will see the advantages that really made this worthwhile. They were able to refinance their mortgage and reduce the interest rate by a percentage point. Thousands of dollars will be saved over the repayment of the loan.

They paid off all of their debts including the car payment of $399.00. This has increased the net income into the home. The amount of equity needed to payoff all of there debts was enough to appear as if they were starting over.

Be On Guard

If you own your home, you might consider a debt consolidation loan. Unlike the first option you read there can be problems. There is a right and wrong way to do a debt consolidation on your home. One kind of loan is a second mortgage on your property, which allows you to consolidate your debts into one payment. Some loan programs require no equity or appraisal. I recommend that if you do not have the equity, do not do the loan.

Most first time buyers end up over their head when they borrow money without equity in their home. It sounds so good when they tell you that you can use this loan to consolidate credit card bills, car payments, and all other bills.

The interest on this loan may be fully tax deductible, depending upon your situation. As with any home loan, this is a lien on your property. If you sell your home, you must pay off both your first and second mortgages. This is an area where many people make their mistakes getting a debt consolidation loan. Without equity in your home, this loan would be considered as a 125% loan. What it actually does is put you upside down in your home. Imagine owing more on your home than what it is worth.

Now, I must admit that there are times that a loan of this type can be an advantage to you. As you learned early savings applied to this loan over a period of time can lessen your liability. Without it, you are surely headed for financial trouble. In addition, although you may be making lower monthly payments, you may be paying for a longer time period than if you paid off each debt individually.

Make an appointment to see a credit counselor. You should be able to find a free service in your area that will help negotiate payments with your creditors, and give you good financial advice. They'll give you a fresh perspective on your financial burden, and help you realize you're not the only one dealing with debt. Sound advice can make the difference. They'll also be candid with you and tell you what options you should consider.

But it is important for you to act. Doing nothing can lead to much larger problems in the future-even bigger debts, the loss of assets such as your house, and a bad credit record. The good news is that there are solutions.

The remedies provided in this book can help improve your relationships with creditors, reduce your debts, and help you manage your money. In brief, these solutions can help give you a new, fresh start. Review your specific obligations that creditors claim you owe to make certain you really owe them. If you dispute a debt, first contact the creditor directly to resolve your questions. If you still have questions about the debt, contact your state or local consumer protection office or state Attorney General.

Contact your creditors to let them know you're having difficulty making your payments. Tell them why you're having trouble- perhaps it's because you recently lost your job or have unexpected medical bills. Try to work out an acceptable payment schedule with your creditors. Most are willing to work with you and will appreciate your honesty and forthrightness.

Each creditor has some type of program available to help you. The problem that I have experienced is that it is hard to talk with the right person. The customer service representative seems very eager to take your head off. And would you believe that in many cases they do not have control over their own money?

Now, the mortgage payment basically remains the same, it however did increase by $50.00 a month. It really did not increase by this amount because of the loan. The increase of $50.00 was because of the plan in place to pay the mortgage off early. They elected to pay this loan over 30 years.

Why such a long period of time? They could afford a 15-year mortgage and pay about $1100.00 a month. But, they felt that it was more important to have a small payment, and to make principle payments to the loan. The additional $50.00 we talked about to the new mortgage payments will allow them the opportunity to pay off the mortgage in less time. You will learn more about my theory of this plan a little later in the book.

That is a great savings right there, but there is also a whole lot more. They increased their tithes to what it should have been. And look at the other areas that they have been able to improve on. They added money to the clothes, personal care, cable, and savings. Savings, this is what I like. They will save $4800.00 a year without interest, if they continue over time 5 years $24,000.00, 15 years $ 72,000.00, and the expected length of time on the new mortgage is reduced.

With continuous savings they would have $91,200.00 without interest saved. What if they had taken the first ten years of savings $48,000.00 put it in a certificate deposit, locked in at 5.8 % interest compounded daily for the next five years, they would earn $16,103.72, with a total of $64,103.72, in 15 years and the continuous monthly payments of $400.00, the total would be over $92,000.00 in 15 years not 19. Easier said than done? Wrong, remember that you are changing the way you understand and deal with money. This is a great way to build a foundation.

Remember, we talk about financial net worth in Chapter 2, look at the difference in the two lessons. Work out the net worth of both families and see the differences. In just five years this family would have saved $24,000.00 not to mention any additional savings they may contribute.

The impact is that the principle payments on the mortgage in the same time period, this is all foundational. I know it may be hard for some to accept, but nothing is at risk for this family. I want to say just three words to you before I go on, because this is what is it about. Provide, Protect, Preserve.

This family added some freedom in their lives. With the $442.00 that is remaining they can save an additional thousand dollars a year for emergencies by using just $88.00 a month. When you look at their budget, it shows $793.00 that would be spent on the family after all bills are paid, including long-term savings.

Last but not least, they will receive a tax break over the whole period. Once they have gotten the foundation in place, they can now look at more aggressive opportunities to invest their money. The key would be to determine how much risk they would want to take on.

This is not about investing in the stock market, it is more about investing in yourself. The only investment plan or programs that we will recommend, will be things that offer security and no risk. Your focus now should not be on investment, especially if you are just really learning how to budget. If you cannot manage your money now, how would you be able to manage an investment portfolio. Unless, you have money to burn.

YOU HEARD THE STORY
"TO TEACH A MAN TO FISH"
SO WHAT EXCUSE DO YOU
HAVE FOR YOURSELF?

Rob Wilson

CHAPTER SIX

CREDIT
WHAT IT REALLY IS...

This I know will not shock you, but when you read this chapter you may want to really revisit the 1st and 2nd Chapters, to refresh your memory about my purpose and your responsibility.

You know of the banking system that we all utilize and have mixed emotions regarding their practices. Well, congressional findings for the purpose of fairness, and impartiality created the Credit Reporting Act. This Act is to ensure the accuracy and fairness of credit reporting.

It is vital in assembling and evaluating consumer credit and other information on consumers. An elaborate mechanism has been developed for investigating and evaluating the **credit worthiness, credit standing, credit capacity, character, and the general reputation** of consumers.

When we talk about credit and what it really is, Do we really want to know? For this moment in time let's think about character, and general reputation. The use of the word character should perturb you. How can they look at a credit report and know your character? Dose it are show your emotions or your personality? How is it able to say anything about you?

Your general reputation, it is possible that this system is able determine my standing or prestige. It this something that you have really taken for granted?

Let me try to answer those questions. The credit scoring system does a number of things. It sets a credit capacity for you that allows creditors to extend credit to you. The capacity is based on the current amount of credit information they may have.

The least amount of information may only provide you a very small amount of credit, if any at all. Contrary, the more information they have can establish a higher line of credit. Once there is a capacity establish in your name it follows you. Based on how you deal with this credit capacity over a period of time helps them to determine your credit worthiness. Your credit worthiness is reviewed in as little as one month and as far back as seven years. The credit worthiness also works together with the credit standing.

Making your payment on time establishes the credit standing. It watches closely how you pay all your bills. It also helps the credit capacity by reviewing the amount of credit you have as it relates to your income. Because of your income you may be overextended with credit. It's funny how we are now talking about credit, and moments ago we were calling it debt. In the first chapter, we talk about the biblical principles of money. As we saw in the scriptures that honesty and trust are some of the principles. The credit system in many ways is based on trust as well.

If we operate in an honest manner, we will never have credit related problems. I do not mean that anyone is dishonesty or has been, but if we sincerely discipline ourselves we would not overextend ourselves. This system so far sounds fair, and for the most part it is very fair. Most of our problems stem from our own inability of understanding the importance of credit. We must be knowledgeable enough to make sound judgment in our financial decisions. It really is not just about finances, it also affects employment, and insurance as well.

If wealth is your desire, it is unlikely that you will obtain it without having consideration of your credit. I truly believe that if you read from the beginning of this book you have different views from when you started. But, if you have skipped around looking for what you feel you really need, you may have missed something very important.

A very dear friend always reminds me, I am the most valuable asset that I will ever have, my ability to earn an income. If my credit affects my employment, than my ability to earn money is diminished greatly. Which will have a direct affect on any hopes of building wealth, just another reason why your credit is so important. Recently, I spoke with a woman who had accepted early retirement from a Fortune 500 corporation. A few years ago, she went though a divorce and filed personal bankruptcy. After a few months off, she begins to look for work.

Time after time she found herself being denied employment. She could not understand why, then after she was turned down on a job that she knew she should have landed, she asked the interviewer why. To great surprise, she was told it was the bankruptcy on her file that disqualified her. She was outraged to find that it was her credit. She was finally able to find a job. But, it did not pay her nearly what she should have been receiving with her qualifications. This has happened many times to people, and they do not have an idea why.

Another interesting case involving credit, was a family that could afford to pay for life and medical insurance. They realized that more medical insurance was needed for their children. This family had a child that required they have additional insurance. Over the years, they had neglected to pay their bills on time each month. The payment was always made, but, it was always thirty days late. When they applied for the insurance, it was denied. The family now will have to pay for the needed medical expense, out of their pocket.

Having to pay an average of $5,000.00 a year for medical expenses really hurts their ability to save money. The same is true with auto insurance, you may receive it, but at what cost. Remember, the point that we are trying to make is simple. There are many areas that have a direct impact on your ability to obtain wealth. Credit cannot be taken lightly.

There are many people who believe that they can create financial wealth without credit. I would like to persuade them differently. Good credit is essential in our society today, because so many of the things that we would like to buy will need to be financed or obtained on credit.

If you want a house, or car, student loans, employment, or simply auto insurance, you will need credit. As we stated earlier, this is personal. So far, I am sure you can see how personal it is. Even I, myself am called the Credit Surgeon. Yet, with all of my knowledge about credit it will not change the fact that it is personal. Many "credit doctors" claim to have an answer for you. Do not fall victim to their false promises.

The main source of information on what you would ever need is available to you free of charge at your local library. You also can go directly to the Federal Trade Commission, and receive this information at no cost. All of this information ties in together. Budgeting, managing your money, understanding your liabilities, and making sound judgments. That is our purpose: to establish the foundation of knowledge in all of these areas. With the right knowledge, you can empower yourself to set a foundation with a determine plan.

Please, do not take credit likely, it will follow you all of the days of your life. Try the simple test below and see how knowledgeable you really are about credit.

Do You Want Positive Credit?

Maybe you've recently come out of a tough credit and/or financial situation like a bankruptcy or maybe you're young and haven't used credit yet. If you've just gotten out from under a bankruptcy or finished paying off a lot of credit cards, you may be tempted to pay for everything in cash, not wishing to repeat your past mistakes.

Many people think having no existing debts is a positive trait valued by lenders. Nothing could be further from the truth. A borrower with no credit is almost as bad as bad credit. A creditor wants to see how you'll handle debts. A person just out of financial difficulty needs to show potential lenders that they have learned their lesson and are now committed to improving their credit habits.

Your credit is about you. If I sold you on anything that I've said, please, let it be that you made a decision that is best for you. It's not tailored for any one person, but it does show you how to do it yourself. "Looking closely at your options can help you realize that we still needed to try self-budgeting before taking more extreme measures. We think that perhaps we were giving up too soon."

Now, if there are late payments and a bad rating, and the account has been paid in full or settled, you can attempt to have the late payments removed and change the derogatory information. Remember, they really don't like doing it, but they will. You are going to have to be compelling in ways that make you uncomfortable. This helps you clear up the problems in the past and jump-start your credit file towards recovery. Whatever you decide, think of your best interest and your future.

When you go to borrow $10,000.00 at a 15 to 25 % interest rate, what is it that makes, some of us feel good about borrowing this much money to pay off $10,000.00? Let's take a look. We finally get caught up with the payments that we are behind on. We now have one single payment to make each month that is much lower than the amount we were required to pay monthly.

I want you to consider, that when you owe thousands of dollars in loans or credit cards regardless of the interest rate, most, if not all of your creditors will accept at least 70% on the dollar. Therefore, knowing this to be a fact and that some will even go as low as 55% on the dollar, why would you even dream of borrowing $10,000.00 to repay $10,000.00?

As a consumer, you can save money just by offering a lower payment and let them make a counter offer. Trust me, they will. Some will be more difficult than others, but you must make the sell. Each bank has a pre- bankruptcy department that will act quickly to settle an open account. It doesn't have to be a closed account to settle. If the account is with a collection agency, you really have two very good options.

Remember, it's up to you to decide, not the collector. If you are not able to offer a settlement, because there is no savings and you cannot borrow it, you can contact the agency and get a feeling of what they will settle for. (It probably will be around 80% on the dollar.)

Then, you listen very carefully. They may even go lower because you did not bite on the first offer. Believe me when I say, that they really want to settle the account. Now, they will be angry, so just make sure that you get the correct address and send them post dated checks. The reason that you will use the arrangement with post-dated checks, is to set the amount that you will pay them. Also, you are setting a goal to save money to allow you the opportunity to make a settlement offer.

The second option is just a little harder. Why? When the account is with your original creditor, they will only settle when the money is in your hands. They are not required to honor post-dated checks the way the collection agency is required by law. They will be taken to the bank the moment they get them. So, you will need to have the ability to borrow the money or take it from your savings. The most effective way is to set a goal before you even contact them. Map out how long it will take and when you will have the money.

Because the account is delinquent, you also can negotiate the rating that they will put on your credit report. As in all cases, always get it in writing before you release your money. Settlements can happen. It's being done every single day. This is how you will be able to see changes in you budget, how there will be money to save, and how you can begin to have the control that you may have lost.

The bank lends money based on your attitude. By paying off what you owe helps change how they consider you. Always remember what your report shows about you. It is your fingerprint in the financial world. The other important thing is that you should not panic. Don't fall for the hype that you may hear from people that have never have had the facts.

With attorneys promoting debt consolidation(Chapter 13), it may be hard to convince you not to file bankruptcy after you have been sued. First, most consumers will panic and avoid answering the suit. This is how the attorney that filed the suit gets his power. The court orders a default judgment, then it is placed on your credit file. This is what allows them to garnish your paycheck.

So, how do you deal with it? The best way is to answer the suit within thirty days. Bank on the fact that the attorney does not want to get a court date (that would take 90 - 180 days in some cases.)

Then you want to set-up a payment plan with the attorney just as you would with a collection agency. If he plays hardball with you, use the letter in chapter twelve. Now you've got the control.

Lien, judgments and collection items can be handled just as you would any other charged off debt. This goes back to changing how your future creditors will consider you. If it's money that you owe, don't try to get out of it. That would only prolong your recovery, and set you back, not your creditor. However, rebuilding a credit report is not a quick fix situation and takes about a year to complete, so don't fall for promises of a "glowing report in a matter of weeks" from credit repair agencies or other scams. Just follow the basic outline presented here.

Clean Up Your Credit Report as Much as Possible

First, you must make sure that your credit report is as clean as you can get it. Begin by obtaining a copy of your credit report and examine it thoroughly for errors. Getting your report in tip top shape will help you out immensely as you begin to apply for new credit. See our section on credit repair for more details on how to fix any errors.

Get New Credit

Once you've cleaned up your credit, you are ready to start building a positive credit profile. Follow any or all of these techniques to stack your report with A-1 listings. But, beware, if you stack too many open accounts, or too many credit inquiries, you will be denied based on debt to income ratio and excessive credit inquiries.

Piggy-Back on a Friend

If you know someone (like a good friend or parent) who has good credit, you can "borrow" his or her good credit listings. This friend must have credit cards, and must trust you enough to allow you to become an "authorized user" on his credit cards. Just have your friend call his credit card company and request that you be placed on his card as an authorized user.

Remember, though, when a new credit grantor goes to review your file, he may insist that the balance on the card appear on your debt to income ratio balance sheet. That shouldn't disqualify you for credit if your income is sufficient and you don't have an excess of debt on your file.

Get a Secured Credit Card

Ask your local bank if they offer secured cards. Many national banks are starting to offer this service. Your past credit is less important with these guys, as you will be opening a savings account to secure the credit line on the card. You can get this card even if you have some bad credit still on your credit file. If you put up $500.00 in a saving account, you will be allowed to charge up to $500.00.

Seek Easy Credit

Many stores extend credit without tremendous regard for the credit standing of the applicant. These stores usually can be found in industries with small products or traditionally high mark-ups. Here are a list of creditors who will often extend credit to those without much credit history:

- Fingerhut
- Radio Shack
- Jewelers
- Furniture Stores
- Tire Stores
- Appliance Stores
- Easy credit Auto Dealers
- Gas Cards

Keep the Accounts Active

Once you've successfully received new lines of credit, it is important to have some activity going on these accounts each month. We don't suggest you pile up large debt, maybe $50 dollars or so in a balance, and pay the minimum. Inactive accounts with a zero balance aren't displaying a tendency to handle existing debts. This is what you want to portray to future loan officers and other creditors. You need to display at least one year of positive credit habits to be taken seriously again, especially by a mortgage company. Start now or you will always be a year or two from a good credit standing.

Evaluate how much credit you can afford.

Before you apply for a loan or for a credit card, take a look at your personal financial situation to make sure you can comfortably repay it. Make up a personal or family budget that lists your monthly expenses and compares them with your after-tax income. You can then judge how much you can afford in monthly payments.

If you feel the payments have to be lower in order to be affordable, you may be able to extend the term of the loan. This will have the effect of reducing the amount of the monthly payments, but be aware that the total amount of interest you pay will be higher.

Be knowledgeable and always read the fine print.

The first step to having a healthy credit record is to find out as much as you can before you borrow money. When you do borrow, find out the conditions of the loan: Can you prepay your installments? Can you reduce the term of the loan without penalty? Can you double up your payments?

Don't be afraid to shop around for the best interest rate - or to ask for a better rate. And always read a loan application thoroughly before you sign; be ready to question anything in it that you don't understand.

Always borrow within your means.

It's always a good idea to have a budget - whether you borrow money or not. A budget helps you keep track of where you're spending money and can help you save, too. And, of course, a budget will tell you how much you can afford to borrow, whether it's a term loan, a personal line of credit, or a credit card. If you feel that the cost of a loan will put too much pressure on your personal finances, then reduce the amount you need to borrow.

Avoid impulse buying.

When you have a sudden urge to buy an item and you reach for your credit card, ask yourself this question: Would I be willing to make this purchase if I were paying with cash? If the answer is no, then be strong-willed and do not purchase the item. If the answer is yes, then ask yourself: Can I afford to make the monthly payments? By taking a moment to ask these questions you change a potential impulse purchase into a considered purchase, which is a good way to help you, stay on track financially.

Know how much credit is costing you.

When you apply for a loan or use a credit card, always find out what the interest rate is and what the total interest cost will be. The longer the term of your loan, the more interest you'll be paying. With a loan, you may find it beneficial to shorten the term and increase the monthly payments so you end up paying less in interest. And some banks will let you make payments weekly or bi-weekly, which can also help reduce the interest cost. With a credit card, the longer you extend your credit card payments, the more interest you'll be paying.

Since you can make payments as often as you like on your credit card, you can definitely reduce the amount of interest you pay the faster and more often you make payments.

Match the credit to the purchase.

Different forms of credit are used for different kinds of purchases. Term loans typically are used to buy "big ticket" items, like a car or a boat or furniture. Credit cards are a convenient way of paying for everyday purchases without the need to carry large amounts of cash. A personal line of credit, like a term loan, can be used for a variety of major purchases, from a vacation to a home renovation. And a residential mortgage is most often used to finance the purchase of a home or recreational property.

How to consolidate your debts.

Some people have different loans to finance their various purchases: one or two term loans and, perhaps, several credit card balances. It's often beneficial, both financially and in terms of record keeping, to consolidate these debts. For example, outstanding balances on credit cards can be paid off with a less costly term loan. And two or three loans can be combined into one, sometimes at a better interest rate.

Build a good credit rating.

Having a good credit rating is valuable, and it's something you'll want to protect. The easiest way to do that is to make sure you repay your loans and make your minimum credit card payments promptly. Don't get behind with your payments and try to avoid a situation where you can't repay your loan.

How to reduce your interest costs.

The cost of credit is mostly in the interest you pay to borrow the money. There are several ways you can keep that cost to a minimum.

In the case of a mortgage or term loan, you can reduce the term, which will increase monthly payments but reduce the total amount of interest paid. Or you can repay the loan more frequently, say weekly or bi-weekly.

Many financial institutions will let you make a lump sum payment on the anniversary date, and that, too, will reduce the amount of interest you pay over the term of the loan. With credit cards, the easiest way to keep your interest cost down is to pay off the balance on or shortly after the monthly due date.

The role of credit bureaus/how to check your credit history.

Credit bureaus keep records on the credit history of individuals and companies. These records are used by lending institutions - banks, trust companies, credit unions, and so on - to determine your creditworthiness. Along with other information you supply, your credit record will be used by the lender in making a decision about your loan and, possibly, the interest rate.

Your credit record cannot be given out to just anyone, but you do have the legal right to see it and to correct any wrong information. Simply look up the number for the credit bureau in your local telephone directory, we placed the main three in the back of this book.

Your credit bureau will be able to give you your credit rating, free of charge. You will be asked to provide the following information: name, address, date of birth, and two major pieces of identification (e.g. social insurance and driver's license).

Don't be afraid to ask for help.

If you think you might have difficulty repaying a loan - because of illness or job loss, for example - don't wait until you are forced to miss payments. Go and talk to the lending officer who authorized the loan and explain your circumstances. You'll be pleasantly surprised at how sympathetic they'll be and, more importantly, at their willingness to make adjustments to help you through a difficult period.

If you would like general advice about credit, you may want to talk to someone at a credit-counseling agency. Most of these agencies are government-run and you can find them in the government section of your phone book.

Debt & Credit Counseling

If you are unable to make satisfactory arrangements with your creditors, there are organizations that can help. Many of them are non-profit organizations affiliated with the National Foundation for Consumer Credit (NFCC). They can provide education and counseling to families and individuals. When a individual want help, a financial counselor with a professional backgrounds in money management and counseling can provide support. A counselor will work with you to develop a budget to maintain your basic living expenses and outline options for addressing your total financial situation.

If creditors are pressing you, a counselor can also negotiate with these creditors to repay your debts through a financial management plan. Under this plan, creditors often agree to reduce payments, lower or drop interest and finance charges, and waive late fees and over-the-limit fees. The right counselor should want to educate you, teach you how to have control. Consider every day someone has to tie your shoes for you. What would happen if one day you had to do it yourself? Be careful not to become dependent on someone else.

What's the best way to correct a mistake on my credit card bill?

Under the federal Fair Credit Billing Act, you have the right to dispute mistake on your credit card bill. You must put your complaints in writing, and you must write to a specific billing error address, which may be different from the address to which you send your payments. Never include a dispute letter with your payment. You can call your card issuer, but if you do not write, you may lose your rights.

How should I handle an unauthorized charge (purchase that I didn't make) if I see one on my credit card bill?

It's extremely important to call your issuer immediately if you see an unauthorized charge; this could indicate fraud. Always report lost or stolen credits cards immediately to your card issuer (follow up in writing) and the local authorities.

How can I protect myself from credit card fraud?

In addition to this safety measure, keep your card and card numbers in a safe place, and report loss or theft immediately to your card issuer and local authorities. Your address and phone number are not required as a condition of purchase with a credit card. Contact the National Consumers' League fraud information Center Hotline at 1-800-876-7060, your local Better Business Bureau, or your state attorney general's office if you have questions or problems.

Under law, what information must a credit issuer disclose to me?

The right to full disclosure of cost and obligation information, including finance charges, annual fees, and other charges, like late payment fees, must be given to you under the Truth-in-Lending Act, a federal law.

Do I have legal rights when I use credit?

Under these federal laws, you have the right to access and dispute information in your credit report, the right to know your credit card costs and obligations, and the right to be free from unfair credit discrimination. You may also have right under state laws.

Why should I care about maintaining a good credit history?

Your credit history is contained in written credit report that shows how you paid your bills over time. Not everyone can review your credit report without your permission.

However, lenders, prospective and current employers, car dealers, landlords, and check guarantee firms can obtain a copy of your credit report and may use it to determine your creditworthiness

What should I do if I find myself becoming financially overextended?

It's important to contact your creditors or a counseling service if there's a problem. Failure to pay your bills on time can result in a negative credit report, which can affect your ability to get financing when you need it. Beware of credit "repair doctors" who claim they can repair your credit report for fee. Instead, consider contracting the Credit Counseling Service for budgeting and credit managing assistance.

What do lenders look at when deciding whether to approve a loan?

Typically, lenders making almost any kind of credit decision will look at a variety of types of information, including one or more credit scores. While there are many kinds of credit scores, the most frequently used are credit bureau risk scores developed by Fair, Isaac. These are commonly known as FICO® scores, although they have different names at each of the national credit reporting agencies.

A score is a number that tells a lender how likely an individual is to repay a loan, or make credit payments on time. When a lender requests a credit report and score from a credit reporting agency, the score is calculated by a "scorecard" or scoring model — a mathematical equation that evaluates many types of information from your credit report at that agency. By comparing this information to the patterns in thousands of past credit reports, scoring identifies your level of credit risk.

The importance of any factor depends on the overall information in your credit report. For some people, a given factor may be more important than for someone else with a different credit history. In addition, as the information in your credit report changes, so does the importance given any one factor in determining your score.

Thus, it's impossible to say exactly how important any single factor is in determining your score — even the levels of importance shown are for the general population, and will be slightly different for different credit profiles. What's important is the mix of information, which varies from person to person, and for any one person over time.

Your score considers both positive and negative information in your credit report. Late payments will lower your score, but having a good record of making payments on time will raise your score.

Your score does not consider your ethnic group, religion, gender, marital status and nationality. These are, in fact, prohibited from use in scoring by US law.

Payment History **What is your track record?**

APPROXIMATELY 35% OF YOUR SCORE IS BASED
Your score takes into account:
Considering the payment information on many types of accounts. These will include credit cards (such as Visa, MasterCard, American Express and Discover), retail accounts (credit from stores where you do business, such as department store credit cards), installment loans (loans where you make regular payments, such as car loans), finance company accounts and mortgage loans.

The information in public record and collection items — reports of events such as bankruptcies, judgments, suits, liens, wage attachments and collection items.

Amounts Owed **How much is too much?**

APPROXIMATELY 30% OF YOUR SCORE IS BASED

The amount owed on all accounts, and on different types of accounts. In addition to the overall amount you owe, the score considers the amount you owe on specific types of accounts, such as credit cards and installment loans.

Length of Credit History **How established is yours?**

APPROXIMATELY 15% OF YOUR SCORE IS BASED

How long your credit accounts have been established, in general. The score considers both the age of your oldest account and an average age of all your accounts. How long specific credit accounts have been established. How long it has been since you used certain accounts.

New Credit **Are you taking on more debt?**

APPROXIMATELY 10% OF YOUR SCORE IS BASE
They really look at how many recent requests for credit you have made, as indicated by inquiries to the credit reporting agencies. Note that if you order your credit report from a credit-reporting agency — such as to check it for accuracy, which is a good idea — the score does not count this. This is considered a "consumer-initiated inquiry," not an indication that you are seeking new credit. Also, the score does not count it when a lender requests your credit report or score in order to make you a "pre-approved" credit offer, or to review your account with them, even though these inquiries may show up on your credit report.

Whether you have a good recent credit history, following past payment problems. Re-establishing credit and making payments on time after a period of late payment behavior will help to raise a score over time.

Types of Credit in Use **Is it a "healthy" mix?**

APPROXIMATELY 10% OF YOUR SCORE IS BASED
Your score takes into account: What kinds of credit accounts you have, and how many of each. The score also looks at the total number of accounts you have. For different credit profiles, how many is too many will vary.

**EVERY CREDIT DECISION
WILL COST YOU.
REMEMBER, YOU CAN GET CREDIT
WITH BAD CREDIT.
THE QUESTION IS WHAT WILL YOU PAY.**

Rob Wilson

CHAPTER SEVEN

ABOUT STUDENT LOANS

The Department of Education's has a default management public awareness campaign, the Department's Debt Collection Service (DCS) will aid you with resolving the default status of student loans.

First, the twenty-five question and answers will start dealing with some of the most common problem you might face. You need to know this information, read it carefully.

Who controls my defaulted student loan?

There is the tendency of any loan type to be assigned to the U.S. Department of Education for collection if other agencies have given up on the debt. However, if your loan is one of the Federal Family Education Loans (FFEL) or Direct Loan, such as a Federal Stafford or a Federal PLUS loans it will usually be maintained by a guaranty agency. If it is a Federal Perkins Loan it may be in collection through the school itself.

How do I verify who holds the collection rights on my loan?

The best sources to verify the agency with the collection rights on your account are:
• your collection notices,
• your school, and
• Federal Student Aid Information Center at 1-800-433-3243

How long do I have to repay my loan once I have finished school?

You typically have 30 days to begin repaying your loan. Exceptions may be granted, but they are rare. You should review your loan contract prior to graduation so that you can prepare a budget for your repayment efforts.

How soon do I have to begin repaying my loan if I never finished school?

The answer to this question may be quite exciting to you. If you never finished school, you may be owed a refund, or at least a reduction in the amount you have to repay. You will be required to provide verification from the school that you did not complete your education due to early withdrawal and that you are due a refund.

Such evidence should include, the total yearly assessed cost of your education, as well as a copy of your financial aid award letter detailing how much from each program listed on the award letter was actually disbursed. You may need to give detail on the percentage of the course that you attended along with the schools refund policy.

How much time am I allotted to pay on a loan that is in default?

Technically, your payment can be called "in-full" immediately, if your loan goes into default. You would also be ineligible for any type of deferment or forbearance. The customer service representatives may not volunteer this information, but most guaranty agencies and the U.S. Department of Education will arrange a payment plan, which is acceptable to you and the agency.

What types of loans can be discharged?

In general, only the following classes of loans qualify for discharge-ability:

- Stafford loan,
- PLUS loan,
- SLS loan,
- National Direct Student Loan
- Perkins loan

In order to see if your loan(s) qualify, contact the U.S. Department of Education to find out if your loan is associated with the Title IV Higher Education Assistance program.

How do loan cancellations work?

You should call the U.S. Department of Education about your particular loan type, but in general, a loan can be canceled if the borrower dies or becomes permanently disabled. Additional variances are allowed in special cases such as:
- fraud on behalf of the school with regard to the training
- if the school closes within 90 days of your attendance
- full-time teaching
- military service.
- Head Start Program Staff Member;
- Peace Corps or VISTA Volunteer;
- full-time law enforcement officer or corrections officer;
- full-time nurse or medical technician
- full-time employee of a public or private nonprofit child or family service agency.

What options do I have with respect to consolidating my loans?

Consolidation loans allow you to combine different types of federal student loans to simplify repayment. Even if you have just one loan, you can also choose to consolidate it.

Even though you may be allowed to consolidate your loans you should take caution and understand that a consolidation may extend your repayments for 20 years. Before you agree to consolidate, do the calculations for yourself. Remember that the higher the balance, the longer that it will take to pay off the loan, consequently, the more interest that you will have to pay as well.

Outside of the consolidation process, you are entitled to pay off the balance on each of your loans, independent of the others. Which means that you alleviate the issue of compounding finance charges.

What if I have filed bankruptcy?

Under certain conditions a loan can be discharged due to bankruptcy. Repayment status and associated payment periods may differ depending upon the date that the bankruptcy was filed. (Note: Laws differ from state to state) You may find out more information about whether your loan is dischargeable by supplying information about your bankruptcy to the agency, which services your loan.

What if I don't believe that my loan should be listed in default?

You should be able to substantiate your claim by providing documentation that your loan should not be in defaulted status. If you cannot provide the necessary documentation, then you should seek to obtain verification from the school or the agency, which assigned the defaulted status.

How Do I Handle Collection Agency Harassment?

Collection agencies must comply with the Fair Debt Collection Practices Act. If you feel that you are abused by one of these agencies, contact the Federal Trade Commission. The collection agency's responsibility is to ensure that you repay the debt.

They may assist you by answering questions regarding loan repayment/consolidation or to facilitate updates in your mailing address or balance status.

Do I have to pay on my loan if I've never received a bill?

It is your obligation to make payment even if you've not received a bill. The debt is a matter of contract between you and the loan agency. The bills are sent to you as a matter of convenience. If you properly update your records, you may correct the bill problem.

What if I am not satisfied with the school I attended?

Contrary to popular belief, your contract with the lender on your loan has nothing to do with the quality of service offered by the school. Your loan is just that, a loan and it is to be repaid. The agency may work with you to deal with issues between the school and its regulating body.

What if I disagree with the balance that I am said to have owed?

If you claim that you have repaid a portion of the loan that is not reflected in your balance or that you have repaid the loan in full, then you should provide copies of the cancelled checks, money orders, etc. used to service the debt. If you claim that your income tax has been held to offset the loan but the amount is not reflected in your balance, then you should send copies of the tax information along with a copy of the offset notice.

Isn't there a statute of limitations on collecting a debt?

According to the Higher Education Act of 1965, there is no time defense for not repaying your debt. The holder of the loan has the right to take legal measure to collect the debt.

What if I run into a situation that prevents me from working?

It should be noted that death and permanent disability are acceptable reasons for not paying a debt. If you are unable to repay your loan due to lack of available resources, you should request a "Statement of Financial Status" as well as gather as much evidence as you can of your inability to repay (i.e. check stubs, loan bills, etc.).

If everything works out, you should be able to work out a repayment plan. If your situation is one such as incarceration, you should seek an "Incarceration Verification" letter from the agency involved and have it signed by an official of the incarceration facility.

Can the loan agency withhold my transcript if I do not pay my bill?

No. There is no law that allows a collection agency to put a "hold" on your transcript. The transcript technically belongs the school, so it is the school's decision as to whether to hold a transcript if a loan is in default.

What if I were too young to know any better when I signed for my loan?

In most cases, a minor cannot enter into a contract, however, the Higher Education Act was amended to address this issue since several students begin college prior to their eighteenth birthday.

When does a loan actually become in default?

Default on a loan is usually determined when you fail to make payments for 180 days (if payments are monthly).

What are the consequences of a defaulted student loan?

Once your loan is assigned to collection because of default, you may experience any of the following consequences while the collection agency attempts to recover the outstanding balance owed:

- you may be subject to having your wages (10 to 15 percent of your disposable pay) [Note: Federal employees face an even more severe penalty]
- your credit rating may suffer
- your income tax refund may be seized, you may be subject to legal action, or you may have to pay hefty penalties in collection costs

Can I obtain another loan if I am in already in default?

The answer is typically "NO." Usually, if a loan is in default, you will not receive any deferments or be entitled to any additional money. The general options available to you are: paying the loan in full, consolidation, making consistent payments, or qualifying for loan cancellation

How does a defaulted loan affect my credit?

A defaulted student loan, just as any other bad debt, can have a tremendous impact on your credit. Once a collection agency begins reporting on a defaulted student loan, it will continue reporting on a monthly basis until the debt is paid in full. A little known fact is that negative information can remain a part of your credit history for seven years.

Can my income tax be withheld to repay a loan?

Unfortunately, the answer is "YES." Student loans are generally guaranteed by the U.S. Department of Education (a government agency), and your income tax is paid out by the U.S. Treasury Department (also a government agency). You can believe that the "Government" will get its money.

Can I be forced to pay the incidental expenses for collection?

As unpleasant as it may sound, you are liable for the costs associated with collecting your defaulted loan. You should contact the agency servicing your loan to address your questions regarding these costs.

Can my wages be garnished?

The answer is a resounding "YES." Up to 10-15% of your disposable income can be garnished. You should address the U.S. Department of Education to find out your specific rights and the steps that you can take to avoid garnishment.

Can I be sued for not repaying my loan?

Yes, you may be sued for not repaying a loan, however, this is usually a last alternative. Therefore, you should make every effort to develop payment arrangements.

Repaying student loans held by the U.S. Department of Education?

The goal of the collection agencies is to get their money, however, you may be able to create an arrangement to consolidate your loan. The U.S. Department of Education has several options for loan consolidation, which will allow you the opportunity to make payment arrangements that work out best for you.

The following information we hope will shed light on some of the confusion that is surrounding what you know about student loans. Please read it very carefully, you may find the help you need in this book. Always remember you are not alone, other are having some of the same experiences that you are having.

Federal Family Education Loans (FFEL), which include Federal Stafford and Federal PLUS loans. When placed in default, these loans are first assigned to a guaranty agency for collection. Periodically, guaranty agencies assign loans to the Department for collection.

Direct Loans. Federal Stafford and **PLUS** loans are also offered through the **William D. Ford Direct Loan Program.** When placed in default, these loans are assigned to the Department's Debt Collection Service.

Federal Perkins Loans. When placed in default, Perkins Loans may remain with the school or be assigned to the Department for collection.

Want To Go To School Free?
Loan Cancellation & Discharge

That's right, you could go to school free. One of the main problems that I have found, it the fact that the guidance counselors are not making this information available to you. Not at the high school or college level, are they telling the students which loans does what.

Imagine that you are a schoolteacher that teaches in a school that receives Title IV funding. In most cases, that is a school in the inner city. And for the last ten years you are paying back your student loans. Something happens and you are now in default. They are now scheduling to do an administrative wage assignment. This assignment can happen anytime after you are delinquent more then sixty days.

You may have been able to receive partial loan cancellation, if you only knew about it. Even the principal or the school administration may not have the facts about how to get the loan canceled. What does this have to do with wealth? Think about it for a moment this could have been money that you have saved. Liability vs. Assets, that is what we are talking about.

Over the years I can know tell you the number of people that I have counsel that should not have repaid their loans. I believe that we all should repay any debt we owe back. But, I am talking about programs that they offer to you. The remaining portion of this chapter will identify the what type of loans and their requirements. If you are headed to college, be sure that you investigate the type of loan you apply for.

All loans received under the Higher Education Assistance program can be canceled in several different circumstances including death or total and permanent disability. If you die, or on or after July 23, 1992 the student for whom a parent received a PLUS loan dies, the obligation of you and any endorser to make any further payments on the loan is discharged.

To verify a death, the servicing agency must have either a death certificate, the obituary, a signed document from your funeral director, or other proof of death that is acceptable under state law. Evidence of a your death should be sent to the agency servicing your loan. If the holder of the loan determines that you are totally and permanently disabled, their obligation and any endorser to make any further payments on the loan is discharged. You cannot be considered totally and permanently disabled on the basis of a condition that existed at the time you applied for the loan, unless your condition has substantially deteriorated later, so as to render you totally and permanently disabled.

The full criteria by which you may qualify for such a discharge are set forth in Department of Education regulations 34 C.F.R. 682.402(e). You may request a disability form by contacting the agency servicing your loan. There are other loans types you may qualify for loan cancellation under the following conditions:

A Stafford, PLUS, or SLS loan disbursed after January 1, 1986 can be canceled in two additional circumstances: **(1) the school you attended falsely certified you ability to benefit from the training given; or (2) the school you attended closed while you was in attendance within 90 days after you withdrew from the school.**

If you received a loan through the FFEL Program on or after January 1, 1986 may qualify for a False Certification Discharge if you (or the student for whom a parent received a PLUS loan) to receive the loan was falsely certified by an eligible school. A student's eligibility to borrow is considered to have been falsely certified by the school if the school:

1) Admitted the student on the basis of ability to benefit from its training and the student did not meet the applicable requirements for admission on the basis of ability to benefit; or

2) Signed your name without authorization by you on the loan application or promissory note. Students who borrowed under the Federal Stafford Loan or SLS loan programs, and who received proceeds of the loan on or after January 1, 1986, may be eligible to have your loans discharged if the school placed an unauthorized student or PLUS your signature on the loan application, promissory note, loan disbursement check or electronic funds transfer authorization.

Misrepresentations, by the school, on the other hand, regarding the school's educational program or its financial or administrative capability, including the school's placement services or the quality of the school's facilities, faculty, or equipment are not part of the process of "certification" of the student's eligibility to borrow and do not entitle you to False Certification

If you received a Federal Direct or FFEL Program Loan on or after January 1, 1986, you may qualify may for a Closed School discharge if you (or the student for whom a parent received a PLUS loan) could not complete the program of study for which the loan was intended because the school at which you (or student) was enrolled, closed while you were in attendance, or you (or student) withdrew from the school, or been on an improved leave of absence, not more than 90 days prior to the date the school closed.

You must not have completed the program of study through a teach-out at another school or by transferring academic credits or hours earned at the closed school to another school. If your loan is discharged, you will not owe any more payments on the loan, and you will get a refund of payments you made in the past. Also, if the loan is discharged, the servicing agency will tell credit reporting agencies that the loan was discharged, and any adverse credit history resulting from nonpayment of the discharged loan will be deleted. In addition, their discharged loan will not prevent you from applying for federal student financial aid.

The full criteria by which you may qualify for such a discharge are set forth in Department of Education. Please contact the agency servicing your loan for additional information regarding Closed School Loan Discharges.

A National Defense Student Loan can be canceled in 2 different circumstances: (1) full-time teaching and (2) military service. Recipients of a National Defense Student Loan disbursed prior to June 20, 1972 may receive partial cancellation of your loan for your service as a full-time teacher in:

1) a public or other nonprofit elementary or secondary school;
2) a public/nonprofit elementary/secondary school serving low-income students;
3) a public/nonprofit elementary or secondary school serving handi-capped children;
4) an institution of higher education; and
5) an overseas DOD elementary or secondary school.

A National Direct Student Loan and Perkins Loan can be at least partially canceled in 4 different circumstances: **(1) full-time teaching; (2) military service; (3) Head Start Program Staff Member; and (4) a Peace Corps Volunteer.** Recipients of a National Direct Student Loan and Perkins Loan may receive partial cancellation of your loan for your service as a full-time teacher in:

1) a public or other nonprofit elementary or secondary school serving low-income students; and
2) a public or other nonprofit elementary or secondary school serving handicapped children.

Recipients of Perkins Loans only disbursed after July 23, 1992 may receive partial cancellation of the loan for your service as:

1) a full-time special education teacher or as a full-time qualified provider of early intervention services in a public or nonprofit program; or

2) a full-time teacher of mathematics, science, foreign languages, bilingual education, or any other field expertise where there is a shortage of qualified teachers.

If you believe they may qualify for some type of teacher cancellation of your loan as described above, you should request one "Request for Deferment, Postponement, or Partial Cancellation of Loan" for each year of your teaching service from any school which participates in the Title IV federal student aid program.

The form(s) should then be submitted to the school principal or district official at which you, and the official school seal or stamp must be applied to each form. If you taught handicapped students, you must also submit information regarding the number and age of those students as well as the nature of their handicaps. You should then return the completed form(s) to the agency, which is servicing your loan.

A Perkins Loan can be at least partially canceled in five different circumstances: **(1) as a Peace Corps or VISTA Volunteer; (2) full-time law enforcement officer or corrections officer; (3) full-time teaching; (4) full-time nurse or medical technician; (5) full-time employee of a public or private nonprofit child or family service agency.**

National Defense Student Loan may receive partial cancellation of your loan of your service in the United States Armed Forces if the loan was disbursed after April 13, 1970 and full-time active service began after June 30, 1970.

National Direct Student Loan and Perkins Loan may receive partial cancellation of your loan for your service in the United States Armed Forces if his/her military service was for a full year in an area of hostilities.

If you believe they may qualify for cancellation for your loan(s) due to your military service as described above, you should send a copy of your DD214 (Discharge form) and letter of explanation to the agency servicing your loan.

National Direct Student Loan and Perkins Loan may receive full to partial cancellation of your loan for your service as a Head Start Program staff member. If you believe that they may qualify for cancellation of your loan(s) due to your service as a Head Start Program staff member should send evidence of your service to the agency servicing your loan.

Perkins Loan receives full to partial cancellation of your loan for your service as a Peace Corps volunteer. If you feel that you qualify for cancellation of your loan(s) send evidence of your service to the agency servicing your loan.

Finally, the obligation to repay your loan may be discharged in bankruptcy. Your obligation to repay Title IV, HEA student loan and grant liabilities can be canceled (discharged) due to bankruptcy under certain conditions.

Discharge of your liability does not discharge the liability of a cosigner or endorser of the debt. In general, dischargeability depends on the amount of time between the date on which a loan or grant liability has been due and/or the date that the bankruptcy was filed.

Bankruptcy laws have changed over the years, and as a result, different periods of repayment have been required depending upon the date that the bankruptcy was filed.

Under current law, a loan or grant liability is discharged by entry of a general discharge order if the first payment came due on the debt at least 7 years before the bankruptcy was filed. Before 1991 amendments, only five years was required.

Any grace periods, forbearance, or deferment must be subtracted from the time elapsed between the first payment due date and the filing date when calculating time in repayment.

Debts outstanding for less than the required seven-year period can be discharged only if the court makes an express finding that the repayment of the debt would place an "undue hardship" on you. These non-dischargeability requirements apply to educational loans received by both student and by parent (PLUS Loans), and apply to loans received by any kind of consumers to pay off prior loans (Consolidation Loans).

To determine the dischargeability of a loan, the agency servicing your loan needs the following three pieces of information from you:

> **The First Meeting of Creditors;**
> **List of Creditors (Schedule A-3); and**
> **Notice of Final Discharge of Debtor.**

Inquiries regarding the dischargeability of a student loan should be directed to the agency, which is servicing your loan.

Repaying Student Loans

If you default on their student loan, the maturity date of each promissory note is accelerated making payment in full immediately due, and you are no longer eligible for any type of deferment or forbearance. However, all guaranty agencies and the U.S. Department of Education (ED) will accept regular monthly payments that are both reasonable to the agency and affordable to you.

For student loans authorized under Title IV of the Higher Education Act, default occurs when you fail to make payments on your loan for (a) 180 days if you repay in monthly installments or (b) 240 days if the payments are due less frequently. During the delinquency period, the lender must exercise "due diligence" in attempting to collect the loan; that is, the lender must make repeated efforts to locate and contact you about repayment.

If the lender's efforts are unsuccessful, it will usually take steps to place the loan in default and turn the loan over to the guaranty agency in their state. Lenders may "accelerate" a defaulted loan, which means that the entire balance of the loan (principal and interest) becomes due in a single payment. Once your loan is assigned to a guaranty agency or the U.S. Department of Education for collection, the following steps may be taken to recover the outstanding balance due:

Credit bureaus may be notified, and your credit rating will suffer; the U.S. Treasury may withhold their payments toward repayment of your loan. You may have to pay additional collection costs; also, you may be subject to Administrative Wage Garnishment whereby the Department will require your employer to forward 10 to 15 percent of your disposable pay toward repayment of your loan; Federal employees face the possibility of having 15% of his/her disposable pay offset by ED toward repayment of the loan through the Federal Employee Salary Offset Program.

Finally, the lender or the guarantor of the loan may take legal action to force you to repay your loan. Once a loan is declared in default, you are no longer entitled to any deferments. In addition, you may not receive any Title IV Federal student aid if they are in default on any Title IV loan.

Resolving Disputes

The Department of Education currently contracts with several collection agencies to administer many of the collection activities of our accounts. Only those accounts that fail to establish and adhere to a repayment arrangement are subject to assignment to a collection agency by the Department's Debt Collection Service. Those accounts assigned to a collection agency may have to pay additional collection costs.

Collection agency employees are trained to comply with the terms of the Fair Debt Collection Practices Act, which governs collection practices by debt collectors. When Debt Collection Service is notified in writing of complaints concerning our collection agencies, we review the evidence and take the necessary action to correct the situation.

You may contact the collection agency that your account may have been assigned to at the address or phone number found on their billing statements for questions concerning loan repayment and loan consolidation, to change their mailing address, or for balance information. If you do not know which collection agency their account may have been assigned to, you should or can contact Debt Collection Service for the agency's address and telephone number.

Most of the loans collected by the Department of Education were made by banks or other financial institutions, and the loan contract with that lender is separate and distinct from your enrollment agreement with the school.

Failure by the school to deliver services under the enrollment contract may give you a claim against the school, but generally that claim against the school does not excuse you from honoring their separate loan contract with the lender. Students bear responsibility for examining before they enroll whether a school offers training that meets their academic and vocational needs.

If you have a claim against a school, you should raise those claims against the school directly or through the state consumer protection licensing authorities. In some instances the Department treats complaints against the school as valid grounds for reducing or cancels your obligation to repay a student loan. For example, the Department can reduce the loan liability for you if you can prove you withdrew from enrollment, and were therefore owed, but did not receive, a refund of tuition and fees.

In cases where you believe that the school owes you or the lender a refund for the portion of your education that you did not complete due to your early withdrawal, you must provide the agency servicing your loan with specific evidence that you were owed a refund.

In those cases where you are able to provide such evidence, the servicing agency needs the following to accurately calculate the amount of the refund you are owed:

The total assessed cost of your education for one year. (Because aid is predicated upon total cost, tuition only cannot be used. Also, the total cost of the course in the enrollment agreement cannot be used as it may cover less than one year or more than one year. Aid is calculated and disbursed on a yearly basis.); a copy of your financial aid award letter.

(Not only must the total amount of Title IV aid be known, but also aid from other sources, such as state grants, institutional loans, scholarships, and PLUS loans); how much from each program listed on the award letter was actually disbursed; the length of the course and how long you attended; and the schools refund policy, or the refund policy of the accrediting agency.

Consolidation loans allow you to combine different types of federal student loans to simplify repayment. Even if you have just one loan, you can also choose to consolidate it. Both the FFEL and Direct Loan Programs offer consolidation loans. There are several advantages to consolidate or rehabilitate your loan.

A Direct Consolidation Loan is designed to help student and parent simplify loan repayment. Even though you may have several different federal student loans, you will make only one payment a month for the loans which are consolidated. All loans discussed in this book are eligible for consolidation. Also, the interest rate on the Direct Consolidation Loan may be lower than what you are currently paying on your loan(s).

After your loan is consolidated through this program, it will be removed from its default status, and credit bureaus will be notified that your account has a zero balance. If you owe no other delinquent or defaulted debts to the United States, you will again be eligible for other federal funds, including FHA loans, VA loans, and Title IV student financial aid funds. A Direct Consolidation Loan gives you several expanded repayment options.

The Direct Loan Program offers four repayment plans that are available to consumers of Direct Stafford, Plus, and Consolidation Loans. If you choose to utilize the Direct Loan Program, you may choose one of the repayment plans listed.

1) The Standard Repayment Plan requires you to pay a fixed amount each month, at least $50.00, for up to 10 years. The length of their actual repayment period will depend on your loan amount.

2) The Extended Repayment Plan allows you to extend loan repayment over a period that is generally 12 to 30 years, depending on your loan amount.

Your monthly payment may be lower than your amount under the Standard Repayment Plan, but you will repay a higher total amount of interest because the repayment period is longer. The minimum monthly payment is $50.00.

3) Under the Graduated Repayment Plan, your payments will be lower at first and then increase every two years over a period of time generally ranging from 12 to 30 years.

The actual length of your repayment period depends on your loan amount. Monthly payments may range from 50% to 150% of what it would be if you were repaying the same total loan amount under the Standard Repayment Plan. However, you will repay a higher total amount of interest because the repayment period is longer than it is under the Standard Repayment Plan.

4) The Income Contingent Repayment Plan bases your monthly payment on your yearly income and loan amount. As your income rises or falls, so do your payments. After 25 years, any remaining balance will be forgiven, but you may have to pay taxes on the amount forgiven.

For additional information concerning Direct Consolidation Loans, you may contact the Servicing Center's Consolidation Department at:

U.S. Department of Education
Consolidation Department
Direct Loan Servicing Center
P. O. Box 1723
Montgomery, AL 36102-1723
1-800-557-7392

A FFEL Consolidation Loan is designed to help students and parents to consolidate several types of federal student loans with various repayment schedules into one loan. With a FFEL Consolidation Loan, you will make only one payment a month.

Under this program, your consolidation loan will be made by a commercial lender. Credit bureaus will be notified that your account has a zero balance, and you will sign a new promissory note that will establish a new interest rate and repayment schedule.

To receive a FFEL Consolidation Loan, you must begin repaying your defaulted loan (that is, three voluntary, on-time, full monthly payments). Depending on the balance due, the repayment period may extend up to 30 years.

If you owe no other delinquent or defaulted debts to the United States, you will again be eligible for other federal funds, including FHA loans, VA loans, and Title IV student financial aid funds. You may also be interested in participating in ED's loan rehabilitation program. After you have made 12 consecutive monthly payments that are both reasonable and affordable, ED will agree to reinsure your loan. You will then be eligible to have the loan purchased by a lending institution.

Once a loan is rehabilitated, it will be taken out of default. The credit bureau reports made by ED will be deleted, you will be able to repay the loan over a 9 year period, and you will again be eligible for additional Federally insured loans. For additional information on Loan Rehabilitation you should contact the agency currently administering your account.

If you are unsure which agency is servicing your defaulted student loan(s), you may call 1-800-4-FED-AID (1-800-433-3243) for an address and telephone number of the agency, which holds the defaulted loan(s). There are four customer service centers located in Washington D.C. (Headquarters),   Atlanta (Region IV), Chicago

(Region V), and San Francisco (Region IX). You may call (800) 621-3115 to inquire about your account regardless of the region your account is assigned to. Additionally, if your account has been assigned to one of the collection agencies contracted by the Department, you may contact that agency concerning questions related to your account.

Once a loan is declared in default, you are no longer entitled to a deferment or forbearance. In addition, you may not receive any additional Title IV Federal student aid if you are in default on any Title IV loan. However, there are several ways in which you may resolve your default status and reinstate your eligibility for additional Title IV aid.

If you have a defaulted student loan, you may receive additional financial aid by: paying the loan in full; consolidating the loan through either the Direct Loan Program or FFEL Program; reinstating your eligibility to receive additional Title IV aid by making six consecutive, timely monthly payments to the servicing agency; and if the loan qualifies for one of ED's loan cancellation or discharge programs your eligibility for Title IV aid will be reinstated.

CHAPTER EIGHT

MORTGAGES

Elimination the Process

How does your credit report look?

a. Have you paid off all delinquent debt?

Regardless of the rating, they want to see that you have paid off all of those delinquent debts.

b. Has your bankruptcy been discharged?

If your bankruptcy (Chapter 7) has not been discharged for at least two years, there will not be any FHA finances.

c. Will your trustee give a release to purchase a home?

On Chapter 13, you will need the approval of your trustee in order to purchase anything of value.

d. What type of consumer statement will you write?

You may have to do a consumer statement explaining why you had the financial problems that you had in the past, and give the impression that you are now in control.

e. Did you get a copy of all three of your reports?

You will have to know what is showing on all of your reports in order to make the right decision.

f. Are you controlling your inquires?

You know too many inquires will hurt like a bad unpaid debt.

g. What is your debt to income ratio?

I know we keep talking about everything that you have to do. I am convinced that the more you hear it, the more you will understand it.

This information must become a part of all of your business dealings. You will be able to use this information in many different ways, so learn it well.

a. Are your debts more than 20% of your income?

If your debt is more than 20%, you are living on the edge. There is no way a mortgage lender will take the time with you. Why do you think there is something called pre- qualifying? They want to know your debt to income ratio.

b. Can you settle these debts? (reduce ratio and save money)

If there are charged off accounts and delinquent accounts, you may want to try and settle these if you have the money to do so.

c. Are there too many open lines of credit?

Now if you have a lot of open retail accounts with 0 balances, the lender will wonder if you are just waiting to go through the closing to go shopping. This could hurt you.

d. Is there a second income?

Do you have an elderly family member that receives an income or has a part -time job? Your husband or wife's income? Any additional income will help to reduce that debt / income ratio.

e. How soon do you foresee debt reduction?

Are you setting a budget to get control of your debt? Be sure to try and make a settlement with as many creditors as possible. By doing so, it will only save you money and help to get you where you will need to be.

Mortgages

What information will you need for your loan officer?

3 Pay Stubs

If you are paid on the 1st & 15th, you will need three pay stubs.

3 Months of Bank Statements

Three statements that will show where the money is coming from.

2 Years of W-2 's or Tax Returns

Your W-2's only if you are a salary employee, but, if you work on a commission basis or if you are self employed, Tax Returns.

Resident

A letter showing your residency and how you made your payments on time. (At least 2 years)

Employment

All underwriters want to see employment at least two or three years at the same job. Some make exceptions as long as you are in the same field.

Utilities

Get a letter from all of your utility companies showing how you have paid all of your debts. Telephone, gas, lights, water, and any other debts that you have.

- Explanation of financial problems
- Explaining why you had difficulty paying in the past.
- Letter showing payment history
- Have your creditors write a letter showing how you are a valuable customer and have paid your debts on time.

A Fee of $300.00

This fee is done in two parts. The 1st is $50.00 for your credit reports (Experian, Equifax, Transunion). Then there is a $250.00 charge for the appraisal.

Now, if you receive a gift from anyone, the loan officer will provide you a letter that will need to be completed before the closing. If you know that a gift is coming forth, then you must be prepared to get that person from whom the gift came from to do two things. They will need to show that they provided you the funds with a personal check and they will need to send a copy of front & back of the canceled check.

Why must you have all of this information? Well look at it this way, when you are asking for anything, you must show that you have the ability to handle whatever you are about to take on. They may want to try and back out for whatever reason. You also will know your problems before they ever meet you.

How To Save Your Home

I recognize that a consumer may have already in many cases given up on keeping their homes. Therefore, as I write this material, my goal is to open up your minds to other possible options.

It may be to your advantage to seek legal counsel right away. But, seek counsel with an attorney that will be familiar with the process. I am not an attorney. The information that you will learn is information that you really should have known previously.

Like all of our self help books, this is designed to give you more control of your finances. You are not alone when it comes to dealing with financial difficulty. So, be encouraged, research, plan, and whatever you do, DO NOT GIVE UP.

Should you file for bankruptcy? Maybe not. Why? I feel that once you read this information, you will find out about some other options that you may have. More and more, I read about people like some of you that ended up filing for bankruptcy only because they had no other options.

BANKRUPTCY

SO NOW YOU ARE ABOUT TO LOSE YOUR. WHY?

There is truly no reason for you to lose your home. Remember, in Chapter Two I talked about your home being a liability as well as an asset to you. Think about this, if you lose your home there is still a need to pay rent. You are going to have to live somewhere.

What good reason can you justify losing your home? You probably can come up with many reason why. If you have read this book from the beginning, you should now have a different perspective about home ownership and the value that is has in your life.

Because I see a great deal of people losing their homes on a monthly basis, this area is of great concern. The primary reason that most people lose their home is due to the lack of understanding its importance, and having a flawed value system.

Provide, Protect, and Preserve should be your focus. Your mortgage payment should never be compromised at any time. For most of us this is the single largest investment that we will ever make. You must protect it. I am not that out of touch that I do not realize there could possibly be circumstances out of your control. But, I will not justify them.

We also talk about four areas that have a direct affect on building wealth. They are **self-awareness, conscience, creative imagination, and independent will.** As you look back on their meaning and impact on your decision-making, you may agree the there is really not a good reason. In chapter one, one of the most important lessons I learned was sound judgment. Sound judgment is really the key to unlocking wealth.

Let's look at the four areas closely again. Self-awareness is the point and time that we know we need to do something, it's when we know what, when and how. Yet we convert our self-awareness to selfishness, selfishness in deciding that this is what I want, right or wrong.

Conscience is the internal guidance system which allows us to sense when we act or even, contemplates acting. We recognize the distinction between right and wrong in regards to one's own conduct.

Creative imagination is the point and time that we are able to justify the things we do or do not do. Take your mortgage. We will put it off to enjoy other things that we want. We take advantage of the grace period that we have when our financial situation indicates we should not.

Independent will allows us to really feel good about the decisions we make regardless of the outcome. It's the ability to act freely without any outside influences. The point in which we stand our ground on all of our decisions.

Curing a default is a voluntary reinstatement of a mortgage when the delinquency is cured if the lender believes there are reasonable prospects that the homeowner will start making timely payments on future installments. Be sure that you receive a promise in writing and that the payment arrangements will reinstate the mortgage. This right to cure may apply to all home mortgages in some states or only to second mortgages or mobile homes mortgages in others.

Negotiating with the lender, refinancing the mortgage, selling the home, or various forms of government assistance apply to an actual foreclosure as well. You may be under pressure to reach a solution, do so quickly.

Warning! Never offer the deed in lieu. Deed in lieu is generally a very bad idea if you have a significant amount of equity in the home. If the home's value exceeds the amount of the indebtedness, you would ordinarily receive this surplus. If you turn the deed over to the mortgage holder, you may forfeit any right to this equity in your home. You may have valid claims or defenses against the creditor by turning over the deed.

PREDATORY LENDING

As a homeowner, it is important that you realize that you can be a target. Like anything that else that can increase you personal assets there are risks. These risks primarily target the elderly. But, in recent years there has been an increase effort to target any homeowner.

Predatory lending has begun to make national news. In every state you here of cases that has forced families out of there homes. I must say that many of these families are both victim and villain. They are villains when they attempted to get something when they knew it should not be possible. And, the predator victimized them.

Many of the foreclosures around this country have had some form of predatory lending present. Congress has held hearings regarding predatory lending. States have adopted new laws that make it a crime to participate in these practices. Yet, banks, finance companies, credit unions, brokers, and mortgage companies have continued to do business as usual.

This section is to educate you on the tactics and practices that they use. Being a homeowner can be a primary source of wealth building for you and your family. I challenge you to learn what is involved in these processes, for you to better protect yourself. Below you will find many of their tricks that are used to draw you in.

I. ORIGINATION OF LOAN

1. Solicitations. Predatory mortgage lenders engage in extensive marketing in targeted neighborhoods. They advertise through television commercials, direct mail, signs in neighborhoods, telephone solicitations, door to door solicitations, and flyers stuffed in mailboxes. Many of these companies deceptively tailor their solicitations to resemble social security or other U.S. government checks to prompt homeowners to open the envelopes and otherwise deceive them regarding their predatory intentions.

2. Home Improvement Scams. Predatory mortgage lenders use local home improvement companies essentially as mortgage brokers to solicit business. These companies solicit homeowners for home improvement work. The company may originate a mortgage loan to finance the home improvements and then sell the mortgage to a predatory mortgage lender, or steer the homeowner directly to the predatory lender for financing of the home improvements. The home improvements are often grossly overpriced, and the work is shoddy and incomplete. In some cases, the contractor begins the work before the three-day cooling off period has expired. In many cases, the contractor fails to obtain required permits, thereby making sure the work is not inspected for compliance with local codes.

3. Mortgage Brokers - Kickbacks. Predatory mortgage lenders also originate loans through local mortgage brokers who act as bird dogs (finders) for the lenders. Many predatory mortgage lenders have downsized their operations by closing their retail outlets and shifting the origination of loans to these brokers. These brokers represent to the homeowners that they are working for the homeowners to help them obtain the best available mortgage loan.

The homeowners usually pay a broker's fee. In fact, the brokers are working for predatory mortgage lenders and being paid kickbacks by lenders for referring the borrowers to the lenders. On loan closing documents, the industry employs euphemisms to describe these referral fees: yield spread premiums and service release fees. Also, unbeknownst to the borrower, his interest is raised to cover the fee. Within the industry, this is called bonus upselling or par-plus premium pricing.

4. Steering to High Rate Lenders. Some banks and mortgage companies steer customers to high rate lenders, including those customers who have good credit and would be eligible for a conventional loan from that bank or lender. In some cases, the customer is turned away before completing a loan application. In other cases, the loan application is wrongfully denied and the customer is referred to a high rate lender. The high rate lender is often an affiliate of the bank or mortgage company, and kickbacks or referral fees are paid as an incentive to steer the customer in this way.

5. Lending to People Who Cannot Afford The Loans. Some predatory mortgage lenders purposely structure the loans with monthly payments which they know the homeowner cannot afford with the idea that when the homeowner reaches the point of default, they will return to the lender to refinance which provides the lender additional points and fees. Other predatory mortgage lenders, whom we call hard lenders, purposely structure the loans with payments the homeowner cannot afford in order to trigger a foreclosure so that they may acquire the house and the valuable equity in the house at the foreclosure sale.

6. Falsified Loan Applications, Unverified Income. In some cases, lenders knowingly make loans to homeowners who do not have sufficient income to repay the loan. Often, such lenders wish to sell the loan to an investor. To sell the loan, the lender must make the loan package have the appearance to the investor that the borrower has sufficient income. The lender has the borrower sign a blank loan application form. The lender then inserts false information on the form (for example, a job the borrower does not have), making the borrower appear to have higher income than he or she actually has.

7. Adding Co-signers. This is done to create the false impression that the borrower is sufficiently credit worthy to be able to pay off the loan, even though the lender is well aware that the co-signer has no intention of contributing to the repayment of the mortgage. Often, the lender requires the homeowner to transfer half ownership of the house to the co-signer. The homeowner has lost half the ownership of the home and is saddled with a loan she cannot afford to pay.

8. Incapacitated Homeowners. Some predatory lenders make loans to homeowners who are clearly mentally incapacitated. They take advantage of the fact that the homeowner does not understand the nature of the transaction or the papers that she signs. Because of her incapacity, the homeowner does not understand she has a mortgage loan, does not make the payments, and is subject to foreclosure and subsequent eviction.

9. Forgeries. Some predatory lenders forge loan documents. In an ABC Prime Time Live news segment that aired on April 23, 1997, a former employee of a high cost mortgage lender reported that each of the lender's branch offices had a "designated forger" whose job it was to forge documents. In such cases, the unwary homeowners are saddled with loans they know nothing about.

10. High Annual Interest Rates. The very purpose of engaging in predatory mortgage lending is to reap the benefit of high profits. Accordingly, these lenders always charge unconscionably high

interest rates, even though their risk in minimal or non-existent. Such rates drastically increase the cost of borrowing for homeowners. Predatory mortgage lenders routinely charge Atlanta area borrowers rates ranging from 12% to 18%, while other lenders charge rates of 7.0% to 7.5%.

11. High Points. Legitimate lenders charge points to borrowers who wish to buy down the interest rate on the loan. Predatory lenders charge high points but there is no corresponding reduction in the interest rate. These points are imposed through prepaid finance charges (or points or origination fees), they are usually 5 to 10% of the loan and may be as much as 20% of the loan. The borrower does not pay these points with cash at closing. Rather, the points are always financed as part of the loan. This increases the amount borrowed, which produces more annual interest to the lender.

12. Balloon Payments. Predatory mortgage lenders frequently structure loans so that at the end of the loan period, the borrower still owes most of the principal amount borrowed. The last payment balloons to an amount often equal to 85% or so of the principal amount borrowed. Over the term of the loan, the borrower's payments are applied primarily to interest. The homeowner cannot afford to pay the balloon payment at the end of the term, and either loses the home through foreclosure or is forced to refinance with the same or another lender for an additional term at additional cost.

13. Negative Amortization. This involves a system of repayment of a loan in which the loan does not amortize over the term. Instead, the amount of the monthly payment is insufficient to pay off accrued interest and the principal balance therefore increases each month. At the end of the loan term, the borrower owes more than the amount originally borrowed. A balloon payment at the end of the loan is often a feature of negative amortization.

14. Padded Closing Costs. In this scheme, certain costs are increased above their true market value as a method of charging higher interest

rates. Examples include charging document preparation of $350 or credit report fees of $150, both of which are many times the actual cost.

15. Inflated Appraisal Costs. This is another padding scheme. In most mortgage loan transactions, the lender requires that an appraisal be done. Most appraisals include a typical, detailed report of the condition of the house (interior and exterior) and prices of comparable in the area. Others are "drive-by" appraisals, done by someone driving by the homes. The former naturally cost more than the latter. In some cases, borrowers are charged a fee for an appraisal, which should include the detailed report, when only a drive-by appraisal was done.

16. Padded Recording Fees. Mortgage transactions usually require that documents be recorded at the local courthouse. State or local laws establish the fees for recording the documents. Mortgage lenders typically pass these costs on to the borrower. Predatory mortgage lenders often charge the borrowers a fee in excess of the actual amount required by law to record the documents.

17. Bogus Broker Fees. In some cases, predatory lenders charge borrowers broker fees when the borrower never met or knew of the broker. This is another way such lenders increase the cost of the loan for the benefit of the lender.

18. Unbundling. This is another way of padding costs by breaking out and itemizing charges that are duplicative or should be included under other charges. An example is where a lender imposes a loan origination fee, which should cover all costs of initiating the loan, but then imposes separate, additional charges for underwriting and loan preparation.

19. Credit insurance - Insurance Packing. Predatory mortgage lenders market and sell credit insurance as part of their loans. This includes credit life insurance, credit disability insurance, and involuntary unemployment insurance. The premiums for this insurance are

exorbitant. In some cases, lenders sell credit life insurance covering an amount, which constitutes the total of payments over the life of the loan, rather than the amount actually borrowed. The payout of claims is extremely low compared to the revenue from the premiums. The predatory mortgage lender often owns the insurance company, or receives a substantial commission for the sale of the insurance. In short, credit insurance becomes a profit center for the lender and provides little or no benefit to the borrower.

20. Excessive Prepayment Penalties. Predatory mortgage lenders often impose exorbitant repayment penalties. This is done in an effort to lock the borrower into the predatory loan for as long as possible by making it difficult for her to refinance the mortgage or sell the home. Another feature of this practice is that it provides back end interest for the lender if the borrower does prepay the loan.

21. Mandatory Arbitration Clauses. By inserting pre-dispute, manda-tory, binding arbitration clauses in contractual documents, some lenders attempt to obtain unfair advantage of their borrowers by relegating them to a forum perceived to be more favorable to the lender than the court system. This perception exists because discovery is not a matter of right but is within the discretion of the arbitrator; the proceedings are private; arbitrators need not give reasons for their decisions or follow the law. A decision in one case will have no prece-dential value; judicial review is extremely limited; a lender will be a frequent user while the consumer is a one-time participant; and injunctive relief and punitive damages will not be available.

22. Flipping. Flipping involves successive, repeated refinancing of the loan by rolling the balance of the existing loan into a new loan instead of simply making a separate, new loan for the new amount. Flipping always results in higher costs to the borrower. Because the existing balance of one loan is rolled into a new loan, the term of repayment is repeatedly extended through each refinancing. This results in more interest being paid than if the borrower had been allowed to pay off each loan separately.

A powerful example of the exorbitant costs of flipping is the case of Bennett Roberts, who had eleven loans from a high cost mortgage lender within a period of four years. See, Wall Street Journal, April 23, 1997, at 1. Mr. Roberts was charged in excess of $29,000 in fees and charges, including ten points on every financing, plus interest, to borrow less than $26,000.

23. Spurious Open End Mortgages. In order to avoid making required disclosures to borrowers under the Truth in Lending Act, many lenders are making "open-end" mortgage loans. Although the loans are called "open-end" loans, in fact they are not. Instead of creating a line of credit from which the borrower may withdraw cash when needed, the lender advances the full amount of the loan to the borrower at the outset. The loans are non-amortizing, meaning that the payments are interest only so that no credit will be replenished. Because the payments are applied only to interest, the balance is never reduced.

24. Paying Off Low Interest Mortgages. A predatory mortgage lender usually insists that its mortgage loan pay off the borrower's existing low cost, purchase money mortgage. The lender is able to increase the amount of the new mortgage loan by paying off the current mortgage and the homeowner is stuck with a high interest rate mortgage with a principal amount, which is much higher than necessary.

25. Shifting Unsecured Debt Into Mortgages. Mortgage lenders badger homeowners with telephone and mail solicitations and other advertisements that tout the "benefits" of consolidating bills into a mortgage loan. The lender fails to inform the borrower that consolidating unsecured debt into a mortgage loan secured by the home is a bad idea. The loan balance is increased by paying off the unsecured debt, which necessarily increases closing costs (which are calculated on a percentage basis), increases the monthly payments, and increases the risk that the homeowner will lose the home.

26. Making Loans in Excess of 100% Loan to Value (LTV). Recently, some lenders have been making loans to homeowners where the loan amount exceeds the fair market value of the home. This makes it very difficult for the homeowner to refinance the mortgage or to sell the house to pay off the loan, thereby locking the homeowner into a high cost loan. Additionally, if a homeowner goes into default and the lender forecloses on a loan, the foreclosure auction sale generates enough money to pay off the mortgage loan. Therefore, the borrower is not subject to a deficiency claim. However, where the loan is 125% LTV, a foreclosure sale may not generate enough to pay off the loan and the borrower would be subject to a deficiency claim.

II. SERVICING OF LOAN

1. Forced Placed Insurance. Lenders require homeowners to carry homeowner's insurance, with the lender named as a loss payee. Mortgage loan documents allow the lender to force place insurance when the homeowner fails to maintain the insurance, and to add the premium to the loan balance. Some predatory mortgage lenders force place insurance even when the homeowner has insurance and has provided proof of such insurance to the lender. Even when the home-owner has in fact failed to provide the insurance, the premiums for the force placed insurance are often exorbitant. Often the insurance carrier is a company affiliated with the lender. Furthermore, the cost of forced placed insurance is frequently padded because it covers the lender for risks or losses in excess of what the lender may require under the terms of the mortgage loan.

2. Daily Interest When Payments Are Made After Due Date. Most mortgage loans have grace periods, during which a borrower may make the monthly payment after the due date and before the end of the grace period without incurring a "late charge." The late charge is often assessed as a small percent of the late payment. However, many lenders also charge daily interest based on the outstanding principal balance. While it may be proper for a lender to charge daily interest when the loan so provides, it is deceptive for a lender to charge daily

interest when a borrower pays after the due date and before the grace period expires when the loan terms provide for a late charge only after the end of the grace period. Predatory lenders take advantage of this deceptive practice.

III.   COLLECTION OF LOAN

1. Abusive Collection Practices. In order to maximize profits, predatory lenders either set the monthly payments at a level the borrower can barely sustain or structure the loan to trigger a default and a subsequent refinancing.

Having structured the loans in this way, the lenders consciously decide to use aggressive, abusive collection tactics to ensure that the stream of income flows uninterrupted. (Because conventional lenders do not structure their loans in this manner, they do not employ abusive collection practices.) The collection departments of predatory lenders call the homeowners at all hours of the day and night, send late payment notices (in some cases, even when the lender has received timely payment or even before the grace period expires), send telegrams, and even send agents to hound homeowners in person.

Some predatory lenders bounce homeowners back and forth between regional collection offices and local branch offices. One homeowner received numerous calls every day for several months, even after she had worked out a payment plan.

These abusive collection tactics often involve threats to evict the homeowners immediately, even though lenders know they must first foreclose and follow the eviction procedures. The resulting emotional impact on homeowners, especially elderly homeowners, can be devastating. Being ordered out of a home one has owned and lived in for decades is an extremely traumatic experience.

2. High Prepayment Penalties. See description in I. 20 above. When a borrower is in default and must pay the full balance due, predatory

lenders will often include the prepayment penalty in the calculation of the balance due.

3. Flipping (Successive, Repeated Refinancing of Loan). See description in I. 22 above. When a borrower is in default, predatory mortgage lenders often use this as an opportunity to flip the homeowner into a new loan, thereby incurring additional high costs and fees.

4. Foreclosure Abuses. These include persuading borrowers to sign deeds in lieu of foreclosure in which they give up all rights to protections afforded under the foreclosure statute, sales of the home at below market value, sales without the homeowner/borrower being afforded an opportunity to cure the default, and inadequate notice which is either not sent or backdated.

There have even been cases of "whispered foreclosures", in which persons conducting foreclosure sales on courthouse steps have ducked around the corner to avoid bidders so that the lender was assured he would not be out-bid. Finally, foreclosure deeds have been filed in courthouse deed records without a public foreclosure sale.

A GOOD DEFENSES MAY DELAY THE PROCESS

A lawyer or some other professional will have to determine whether lenders have fully complied with all the required procedures and whether defenses to foreclosure are available. There is scrutiny of state statutes establishing foreclosure procedures and judicial decisions interpreting those statutes.

Examples of possible defenses include but not limited to:

• The failure to give proper notice to the homeowner.
• Failure to properly advertise the sale.
• The failure to introduce the original note in the foreclosure proceeding
• The lenders discouraging bid at the foreclosure sale.

Late payment on a mortgage generally triggers the creditor's right to "accelerate" the loan or to call in the full amount of the mortgage due immediately. Failure to pay the full amount then leads to foreclosure.

If the lender surprises the homeowner by suddenly calling a loan in, the lender has been lenient in accepting late payments in the past. If a lender habitually accepts late payments, it must warn you before it calls the whole loan in and attempts a foreclosure.

A NOTICE OF AVAILABLE COUNSELING

The law requires that, for all mortgages, the lender must send the homeowner a notice of the availability of financial counseling, prior to any foreclosure action on principal dwelling.

A notice must be sent whenever the delinquency is due to an involuntary loss or reduction of employment of either you the homeowner or any person contributing to the homeowner's income. Federal law believes that failure to give this notice may prevent the lender from foreclosing on the property. They often send this notice after you have been late only once, and many times it goes unnoticed.

FHA approved nonprofit counseling agencies are listed by the federal government. This generally includes community action programs, consumer credit counseling organizations, and government offices. HUD provides grants to counseling agencies to support their counseling programs.

There is a special protection that applies to the following seven type of mortgages:

- FHA and HUD mortgages
- VA mortgages
- Farmers Home(FmHA) mortgages
- Second mortgages and first mortgages not used to purchase the home (Truth in Lending rescission)

- Liens and mortgages resulting from a home improvement scam
- Mortgages based on unconscionable loan transactions; and
- Where the creditor has no mortgages, but is foreclosing based on a court judgment

WHAT RIGHTS DO YOU HAVE?

- Lenders should give notice of default no later than the end of the second month of delinquency;
- Lenders should make reasonable efforts to arrange face-to-face interviews with homeowners before three full monthly installments are due and unpaid;
- Lenders should accept partial payments in many circumstances;
- Lenders cannot foreclose if the only default is an inability to pay in a lump sum or an escrow shortage;
- Lenders cannot foreclose on the mortgage until you are delinquent on three full monthly payments;
- Before the lender forecloses, you can ask the federal Department of Housing and Urban Development (HUD) to accept "assignment" of the mortgage.
- If HUD accepts the assignment, it takes over the mortgage and temporarily reduces or excuses mortgage payments
- Lenders can't foreclose while a request for an assignment is pending.

VA - GUARANTEED MORTGAGES (FORECLOSURE)

With a mortgage insured by the Veterans' Administration (VA) you also have rights that are not available to other homeowners with a private conventional mortgage. With a VA mortgage there is certain protections against foreclosure for homeowners.

- The lender cannot foreclose unless you have fail to make three full monthly payments.
- The lender must give 30 days warning of its intent.

- The lender must make all reasonable efforts at forbearance before foreclosing.
- They must consider temporary suspension of payments.
- They must consider loan extension or accept partial payments.
- The lender must accept all delinquent payments, late charges, and foreclosure expenses.

TRUTH IN LENDING RESCISSION

You as a homeowner, have an extraordinary means to stop a foreclosure provided by the federal law. Not only does this give you more time to make reduced payments, the federal law allows you to permanently cancel the mortgage and significantly reduce the amount of the debt owed to the creditor.

This remedy is called the Truth in Lending rescission. It is not available to cancel a first mortgage used to purchase a home. But it may be available to cancel other types of mortgages, such as second mortgages, first mortgages not used to purchase a home, and even liens placed on the home by contractors or other workers. Truth in Lending rescission is most effective when dealing with onerous credit contracts imposed by home improvement contractors, finance companies, and mortgage companies that prey on families in financial distress.

We talked about the mortgage loan without equity in the property. Even thought the Truth in Lending rescission sounds almost too good to be true, there are three catches.

- Truth in Lending rescission does not apply to certain types of loans.
- The creditor must have made one of a list of basic mistakes when signing you up for the mortgage.
- You must usually go to court to persuade the lender to honor your Truth in Lending rescission rights.

The Truth in Lending rescission is very technical. We recommend that legal counsel must carefully analyze the law. This is an attempt to make you aware of this law, it may or may not be an option for you. There is an exception when you buy the home.

However, The Truth In Lending Act rescission does not apply if;

- The creditor has not taken an interest in your home and the law does not give the creditor such an interest;
- The mortgage loan was used to purchase the home;
- The mortgage loan was not for consumer purposes, but was for business or agricultural purposes;
- The creditor was only involved in a few loans within the last year.
- The mortgage is on investment property, a vacation house, or other property not your principal residence at the time the loan was extended. (A mobile home, condominium, cooperative, two or three-family home, trailer, even a houseboat can be a principal residence);
- Consumer no longer owns the home that the mortgage relates to.
- The mortgage is a refinancing of an existing loan where no new money is borrowed and the same property stays mortgaged;
- Possibly if the loan was extended more than three years ago (some courts allow consumers to defend foreclosures through TILA rescission even if a loan is more than three years old).

The most important exceptions will be for mortgages used to purchase the home and the possible exception for loans more than three years old. Otherwise, TILA rescission is usually applicable. The key question is did the creditor make a mistake? If so, this will allow you to cancel the mortgage.

You can rescind for any reason within three days of first taking out a loan that uses your home as collateral. This obviously will have little reverence in most foreclosure situations, but is very useful when dealing with high-pressure lenders and home improvement salesman.

You can also cancel a mortgage loan if you never received proper notice that you could rescind the loan. Creditors must deliver two copies of the notice of the right to rescind. The notice must be on a separate document that identifies the transaction, discloses that the creditor has a mortgage on your specified property, and that you and joint owners have a right to rescind.

The notice must also give directions on how to rescind, with a form for that purpose, with the appropriate addresses, the effects of rescission, and how long you have to rescind.

Failure to include all this information or your failure to receive the notices are grounds for you to cancel the loan. As long as you never receive the correct notice, you have a continuing right to cancel the loan (at least for the first three years).

Now, if the creditor makes a mistake in its disclosure of certain important terms of the loan, you may also cancel it. If the disclosure is improper, you can rescind the loan until you receive proper or a corrected disclosure. Although most lenders rarely correct their mistakes. You can cancel even days before a foreclosure if the loan is less than three years old.

If the creditor has made a mistake on the disclosure form, such as the following can be sufficient to allow you the right to cancel.

• Open end line of credit
• The disclosures that have to be correct are the annual percentage rate.
• The method of determining the finance charge and the balance upon which a finance charge will be imposed
• The amount/method for determining any fees and payment information.

For loans that have are fixed payments (a closed end loan), an error in any of the following is grounds to cancel.

• The annual percentage rate
• The finance charges
• The amount financed
• The total number of payments
• The payment schedule.

ERRORS IN THE TRUTH IN LENDING

Any decision to pursue Truth in Lending rescission should be approved by an attorney or other professional experienced with financial calculations and Truth in Lending issues. In fact, the analysis necessary to uncover creditor mistakes may be intimidating for many.

Nevertheless, there are several steps even the most math phobic counselor can take to explore whether your home can be saved through Truth in Lending rescission. Have someone that you are comfortable with and know how to use a financial calculator to check the numbers.

Considering the payment schedule, is the total numbers of payments accurate? Is the annual percentage rate calculation correct? Does the amount financed and finance charges add up to the total numbers of payments? The Truth in Lending law can help to explain what mathematical errors to look for and how to show that the creditor made a mistake.

As a general rule, there is likely to be a creditor error in an extremely high interest rate loan, such as one from a home improvement contractor, finance company, or mortgage company, than in a low interest bank loan. Another reason to concentrate on high interest is that you benefit the most from cancellation of those loans.

Be sure to look for broker's fees, points, insurance, assorted fees, and the like. Always be suspicious if most of the amount financed does not go to the borrower or for the borrower's benefit.

Congress feels that consumers need protection from unnecessarily high settlement charges caused by certain abusive practices that have developed in some areas of the country. Some of the practices Congress was concerned with are discussed below. Most professionals in the settlement business provide good service and do not engage in these practices.

Prohibited Fees. It is illegal under for anyone to pay or receive a fee, kickback or anything of value because they agree to refer a settlement service business to a particular person or organization.

For example, your mortgage lender may not pay your real estate broker $250.00 for referring you to the lender. It is also illegal for anyone to accept a fee or part of a fee for services if that person has not actually performed settlement services for the fee. For example, a lender may not add to a third party's fee, such as an appraisal fee, and keep the difference.

Permitted Payments. Federal laws does not prevent title companies, mortgage brokers, appraisers, attorneys, settlement/closing agents and others, who actually perform a service in connection with the mortgage loan or the settlement, from being paid for the reasonable value of their work.

If a participant in your settlement appears to be taking a fee without having done any work, you should advise that persons company of the RESPA referral fee prohibitions. You may also speak with your attorney or complain to a regulator.

Penalties. It is a crime for someone to pay or receive an illegal referral fee. The penalty can be a fine, imprisonment or both. You may be entitled to recover three times the amount of the charge for any settlement service by filing a private lawsuit. If you are successful, the court may also award you court costs and your attorney's fees.

Your Right to File Complaints Private Lawsuits

If you have a problem, the best place to have it fixed is at its source [the lender, settlement agent, broker, etc.] If that approach fails and you think you have suffered because of a violation of federal and state law you may be entitled to sue in a federal or state court. This is a matter you should discuss with your attorney.

Government Agencies. Most settlement service providers are supervised by a governmental agency at the local, state and/or federal level. Your state's Attorney General may have a consumer affairs division.

If you feel that a provider of settlement service has violated these or any other law, you can complain to that agency or association. You may also send a copy of your complaint to the HUD Office of Consumer and Regulatory Affairs. The address is listed in the Appendix.

Servicing Errors. If you have a question any time during the life of your loan, state and federal laws requires the company collecting your loan payments to respond to you.

Finally, Ask For An Itemization Of The Amount Financed

**EDUCATION COST...THE LACK OF
EDUCATION COST...UNDER
EDUCATED COST...MISS EDUCATED
REALLY COST...CHOOSE WISELY...**

Rob Wilson

CHAPTER NINE

BILL COLLECTORS

How to tell when creditors are violating the law

Laws prohibit debt collectors from using abusive or deceptive tactics to collect a debt however many collectors ignore the law. These guidelines are specifically identified in the Fair Credit Act. This list of questions may help you identify instances when creditors flaunt the law and how you can protect yourself.

1. Can a collection agency call you all hours of the day and night?
2. I'm also getting calls from the collections department of a local merchant I did business with. Can I tell that collector to stop contacting me?
3. A bill collector insisted that I wire the money I owe through Western Union. Am I required to do so?
4. Can a collection agency add interest to my debt?
5. A collection agency sued me and won. Now what happens?
6. What can I do if a bill collector/creditor violates the Fair Debt Collection Act? Collection agencies cannot call you all hours of the day and night.

It's against the law for a bill collector who works for a collection agency (as opposed to working in the collections department of the creditor itself) to call your office or your home before 8 a.m. or after 9 p.m., address you in an abusive manner, harass you making false or misleading statements, adding unauthorized charges, or calling to your family or friends in an attempt to collect your debt.

The law, the federal Fair Debt Collection Practices Act (FDCPA) states that you can demand that the collection agency stop contacting you, except to tell you that collection efforts have ended or that the creditor or collection agency will sue you. However, you must put your request in writing.

I'm getting calls from the collections department of a local merchant I did business with.

Can I tell that collector to stop contacting me?

No. The FDCPA applies only to bill collectors who work for collection agencies. While many states have laws prohibiting all debt collectors—including those working for the creditor itself—from harassing, abusing or threatening you, these laws don't give you the right to demand that the collector stop contacting you. There is one exception: residents of New York City can use a local consumer protection law to write any bill collector and say "stop!"

A bill collector insisted that I wire the money I owe through Western Union. Am I required to do so? Tell them "nice try." In other words no. It's only going to add more money to your debt if you do. Many collectors, especially when a debt is more than 90-days past due, will suggest several "urgency payment" options, including: Sending money by express or overnight mail. This will add at least $10 to your bill. A first class stamp is fine.

Wiring money through Western Union's Quick Collect or American Express' Moneygram is another $11.50 wasted. By putting your payment on a credit card not charged to its maximum, you'll never get out of debt. Be very careful about give your check information over the telephone.

Can a collection agency add interest to my debt?

Yes. The FDCPA allows a collector to add interest if your original agreement calls for the addition of interest during collection proceedings or the addition of such interest is allowed under state law. Every state authorizes the collection of such interest.

A collection agency sued me and won. Now what happens?

Before obtaining a court judgment, a bill collector generally has several ways of getting paid: demand payment, to call you and send you threatening letters, and suing you. Once the collector (or creditor) does sue and get a judgment, however, you can expect more aggressive collections actions:

If you have a job, the collector will try to garnish up to 25% of your net wages. The collector may also try to seize any bank or other deposit accounts you have. If you own property (real estate), the collector will probably record a lien, which will have to be paid when you sell or refinance your property. Remember, there's no statute of limitations on debts. You owe until you pay or file bankruptcy.

What can I do if a bill collector/creditor violates the Fair Debt Collection Act?

First, try to get the collector back on the phone and repeat whatever was said the first time that caused the collector to make the illegal statement(s). Have a witness listen in on an extension or tape the conversation. Taping is permitted without the collector's knowledge in all states except California, Connecticut, Delaware, Florida, Illinois, Maryland, Massachusetts, Michigan, Montana, New Hampshire, Pennsylvania and Washington. Then file a complaint. You can even file a complaint if you don't have a witness, but a witness helps.

The next steps:

1. File your complaint with Federal Trade Commission

2. Complain to your state consumer protection agency.

3.Finally, send a copy of your complaint to the creditor who hired the collection agency. If the violations are severe enough, the creditor may stop the collection efforts.

4.If the violations are ongoing, you can sue a collection agency (and the creditor that hired the agency) for up to $1,000 in small claims court for violating the FTC regulations. (Note: You probably won't win if you can prove only a few minor violations.) If the violations are outrageous, you can sue the collection agency and creditor in regular civil court.

Why a bill collector should not intimidate you?

This book is designed to give you a more in-depth understanding regarding a bill collector's communication with you. If you have ever received a call from a bill collector, you may be spoken to as if you have stolen something or have done something wrong. Consequently you know it can be an intimidating moment when someone is demanding that you pay now.

In any situation, their goal is to capitalize on you not realizing how the law protects you from such behavior. The Fair Debt Collection Practice Act (F.D.C.P.A.) was designed to govern every time a collector attempts to communicate with you. I must point out that the collection industry does not necessarily train collectors to violate the law, but it does however approve and insist on an aggressive approach.

After being a successful bill collector myself, as well as having trained bill collectors, I will admit that we train them to know how close to come to that gray line. They would ask questions and make statements that you may interpret as misleading or implying.

Examples:

If you fail to have your payment in my office by Monday, your paycheck may be garnished.

You have 24 hours to give me a call back before the account possibly goes to litigation.

We will contact payroll and send a garnishment order.
I am the senior auditor, this is a last attempt to resolve this matter.

I'm calling regarding a possible legal matter.

Each of these statements changes your mindset regarding the true status of your account. A well trained bill collector would never let you off the hook. The following information contains some of the major points on the collection procedures most agencies use to collect a bad debt.

Bill collectors attempt to create a level of urgency by the type of letters that they will send you.

- **Asset Investigation Letter** - This letter threatens to get certain financial information regarding you.
- **Strong Demand Letter** - This letter states that payment is due now.
- **Broken Promise Letter** - This approach is to try to motivate you.
- **Final 15** - Day Demand Prior to Legal - This states that time is approaching a dead line.
- **Last Ditch Letter to Establish Partial Payment Arrangements** - They want anything that you will send.

Closed-ended questions used to do the following:

- Narrowing the options you may have to bring you to the point of agreement or to have you draw a conclusion they want.
- Making a statement of support and tagging a question on the end.
- They will use a series of small "yes" questions, and they will lead you to a major "yes" answer (as in a payment).
- Turning your statements into a question in order to get you to elaborate further.
- They will offer you two answer choices instead of just one to keep you on track and/or nail you to a specific answer.

In the following pages you will find the F. D. C. P. A. This law was designed for your protection. We have given the interpretation from my point of view as a former bill collector. This interpretation is widely taught to bill collectors but not practiced.

The F. D. C. P. A act to amend you Credit Protection Act to prohibit abusive practices by debt collectors. Be it enacted by the Senate and House of Representatives of the United States of America in Congress assembled, your Credit Protection Act (15 U. S. C. 1601 et seq.) is amended by adding at the end thereof the following new title:

TITLE VIII DEBT COLLECTION PRACTICES

Sec: 801. Short Title
802. Finding and purpose.
804. Acquisition of location information.
805. Communication in connection with debt collection.
806. Harassment or abuse.
807. False or misleading representations.
808. Unfair practices.
809. Validation of debts.

SECTION 801 SHORT TITLE

801 Text "This title is cited as the 'Fair Debt Collection Practices Act'."

SECTION 802 FINDINGS AND PURPOSE

802 Text "(a) There is abundant evidence of the use of abusive, deceptive and unfair debt collection practices by many debt collectors. Abusive debt collection practices contribute to the number of personal bankruptcies, to marital instability, to the loss of jobs, and to invasions of individual privacy. (b) Existing law and procedures for redressing

these injuries are inadequate to protect consumers. (c) Means other than misrepresentation or other abusive debt collection practices are available for the effective collection of debts.

(d) Abusive debt collection practices are carried on to a substantial extent in interstate commerce and through means and instrumentalities of such commerce. Even where abusive debt collection practices are purely intrastate in character, they nevertheless directly affect interstate commerce. (e) It is the purpose of this title to eliminate abusive debt collection practices by debt collectors, to insure that those debt collectors who refrain from using abusive debt collection practices are not competitively disadvantaged and to promote consistent state action to protect consumers against debt collection abuse."

SECTION 804 ACQUISITION / LOCATION INFORMATION

804 Text. "Any debt collector communicating with any person other than you for the purpose of acquiring location information about you shall, identify himself, state that his is confirming or correcting location information concerning you, and, only if expressly requested, identify his employer;"

Explanation

They can give the person their name, but do not have to give the name of their employer unless they are specifically asked.

Example of Violations

1. Giving the name of his or her company to someone other than you without being asked.

2. Giving the name of a company they are not employed by when asked who their employer is.

3. Pretending they are with another firm or giving false reason for needing to locate you (such as "I have a package I need to deliver," or "She has won a prize.")

804 Text. "The collector shall not state that such consumer owes any debt;"

Explanation

They should not give any indication that they are calling concerning a debt. They should only say, "I'm calling concerning a personal business matter."

Example of Violations

1. Any statement or implication that the call is debt related.
2. Any statement or implication that would embarrass you.

804 Text. "The collector shall not communicate with any such person more than once unless requested to do so by such person or unless the debt collector reasonably believes that the earlier response of such person is erroneous or incomplete and that such person now has correct or complete information;"

Explanation

They cannot recall the third party unless the information they provided was wrong, such as a phone number, and they wish to get the correct number. If they believe they have additional or more current information regarding your whereabouts at a later date, they may recall them.

Example of Violations

Repeated calls to irritate the called party in an attempt to cause you problems or coerce payment.

804 Text. "The collector shall not communicate by post card;"

Explanation

Post cards may not be used in skip tracing.

Example of Violations

Sending any open-faced mail for the purpose of locating you.

804 Text "The collector shall not use any language or symbol on any envelope or in the contents of any communication effected by the mails/ telegram that indicates that the debt collector is in the debt collection business or that the communication relates to the collection of a debt."

Explanation

Written communication on the outside of the envelope should not indicate that they are a collection agency.

Example of Violations

A letter that indicates it's a debt to cause embarrassment or coerce payment.

804 Text. "Once the debt collector knows you are represented by an attorney with regard to the subject debt and has knowledge of, or can readily ascertain, such attorney's name and address, not communicate with any person other than that attorney, unless the attorney fails to respond within a reasonable period of time to communication from the debt collector."

Explanation

If they know or have reason to know that an attorney represents you they must direct all communication to your attorney.

Example of Violations

Continuing to call you when they know that an attorney represents them.

SECTION 805 COMMUNICATION IN CONNECTION WITH DEBT COLLECTION

805 (a) Text. "Without the prior consent of you given directly to the debt collector or the express permission of a court of competent jurisdiction, a debt collector may not communicate with a consumer in connection with the collection of any debt.

• at any unusual time or place or a time or place known or which should be known to be inconvenient to you. In the absence of knowledge of circumstances to the contrary, a debt collector shall assume that the convenient time for communicating with a consumer is after 8 o'clock antemeridian and 9 o'clock postmeridian, local time at your location.

• if the debt collectors know you are represented by an attorney with respect to such debt and has knowledge of, or can readily ascertain, such attorney's name and address, unless the attorney fails to respond within a reasonable period of time to a communication from the debt collector or unless the attorney consents to direct communication with you; or

• at your place of employment if the debt collector knows or has reason to know that your employer prohibits you from receiving such communication."

Explanation

They can only communicate with you between 8 a.m. and 9 p.m. local time. Calls may be made at other hours if permission is given directly by you.

However, they should not call at any time that they know is inconvenient to him/her. They cannot call you if they know that an attorney is representing you. No calls should be made to your work place if calls are prohibited.

Example of Violations

Calling before 8 a.m. or after 9 p.m.
Calling when they know you are sleeping.
Calling you when they know you are represented by an attorney.
Repeated calls to your job after they find out no calls allowed.
Calling you collect without disclosing their name, company name and client's name.

805 (b) Text. "COMMUNICATION WITH THIRD PARTIES except as provided in section 804, without the prior consent of you given directly to the debt collector, or the express permission of a court of competent jurisdiction, or as reasonably necessary to effectuate a post judgment judicial remedy, a debt collector may not communicate, in connection with the collection of any debt, with any person other than you, his attorney, a consumer reporting agency if other wise permitted by law, the creditor, the attorney of the creditor, or the attorney of the debt collector."

Explanation

They cannot discuss the debt with anyone other than the persons responsible for repayment unless you personally authorize them to do so.

Example of Violations

Discussing the debt with the mother or father, relative, or any other person without your permission.

805 (c) Text. "CEASING COMMUNICATION If a consumer noti-fies a debt collector in writing that he/she refuses to pay a debt or that he/she wishes the debt collector to cease further communication with them, the debt collector shall not communicate further with you with respect to such debt, except to advise you the debt collector's further efforts are being terminated;

1. To notify you that the debt collector or creditor may invoke specified remedies which are ordinarily invoked by such debt collector/creditor;

2. Where applicable, to notify you that the debt collector or creditor intends to invoke a specified remedy. If such notice from you is made by mail, notification shall be complete upon receipt."

Explanation

Upon receipt of written notice from you to cease communication, they may make one more contact with you to advise you of the action they plan to take (by mail or phone). After that they cannot contact you again.

Example of Violations

Contacting a consumer more than once after they receive a written request to cease communication.

805 (d) Text. "For the purpose of this section, the term 'consumer' includes your spouse, parent (if you are a minor), guardian, executor."

Explanation

They may discuss the debt with any of these individuals who are responsible for repayment.

Example of Violations

Discussing the debt with the parents of an adult consumer. They cannot discuss the debt with anyone other than you without expressed permission.

SECTION 806 HARASSMENT OR ABUSE

806 Text. "A debt collector may not engage in any conduct the natural consequence of which is to harass, oppress, or abuse any person in connection with the collection of a debt. Without limiting the general application of the foregoing, this conduct is a violation of this section."

806 Text. The following conduct is a violation. "The use or threat of use of violence or other criminal means to harm the physical person, reputation or property of any person."

Explanation

They cannot threaten to harm you or any person in any shape, or form.

Example of Violations

Threats of violence to you or any person.
Threats to destroy property.
Threats to harm reputation.
Indirectly implying or using deceptive means to coerce payment.
Using any criminal means to coerce payment.

806 Text. The following conduct is a violation. "The use of obscene or profane language or language the natural consequence of which is to abuse the hearer or reader."

806 Text. The following conduct is a violation. "The publication of a list of consumers who allegedly refuse to pay debts, except to a consumer reporting agency or to persons meeting the requirements of section 603(f) or 604 of this act."

Explanation

A list of consumers is not provided to anyone for any reason. Only creditors have access limited to their consumer account and records.

Example of Violations

Providing lists of consumers as a means of "black balling" them.

806 Text. The following conduct is a violation. "Causing a telephone to ring or engaging any person in telephone conversation repeatedly or continuously with intent to annoy, abuse, or harass any person at the called number."

Explanation

Any activity that harasses and abuses is prohibited.

Example of Violations

When a collector calls a consumer back immediately after he/she has hung up on them. Leaving repeated messages on an answering machine to annoy consumer. When a collector calls a consumer every day or several times each week with intent to coerce payment through abuse.

806 Text. The following conduct is a violation. "Except as provided in section 804, the placement of telephone calls without meaningful disclosure of the caller's identity."

Explanation

A collector should always give their name and company name when communicating with a consumer. When speaking with someone other than you, they should give only their name but, if expressly asked, give company name. Use only one alias name consistently.

Example of Violations

Giving a company name other than the true company name.
Not giving their name in an attempt to harass.
Using multiple alias names.

SECTION 807 FALSE/MISLEADING REPRESENTATIONS

807 Text. "A debt collector may not use any false, deceptive or misleading representation or means in connection with the collection of any debt. Without limiting the general application of the foregoing, the following conduct is a violation of this section."

807 Text "The false representation or implication that the debt collector is vouched for, bonded by, or affiliated with the United States or any state, including the use of any badge, uniform, or facsimile thereof."

Explanation

They cannot falsely imply they are affiliated in any way with government or law enforcement agencies. They cannot say anything that is not the truth.

Example of Violations

Saying they are collecting a student loan for the government.
Impersonating any government official or department.

807 (A) Text. The following conduct is a violation. "The false representation of the character, amount, or legal status of any debt.

Explanation

They cannot falsely represent the current status of the debt.

Example of Violations

1) Knowingly giving an incorrect balance.
2) Representing that a lawsuit has been filed when it has not.
3) Any false statements about the account and its status.

807 (B) Text. The following conduct is a violation. "The false representation of any services rendered or compensation which may be lawfully received by any debt collector for the collection of a debt."

Explanation

They prohibit informing you that he/she will be required to pay collection or additional costs if it is illegal to add these charges.

Example of Violations

Threatening or adding any unlawful amounts to the debt.

807 Text. The following conduct is a violation. "The false representation or implication that any individual is an attorney or that any communication is from an attorney."

Explanation

They cannot state or imply that they are with a law firm or are an attorney.

Example of Violations

Using "legal" terminology to make you think they are an attorney.

807 Text. The following conduct is a violation. "The threat to take any action that cannot legally be taken or that is not intended to be taken."

Explanation

Owing a debt is not a criminal matter and therefore is not punishable by imprisonment. The collector cannot threaten to do anything they cannot legally do, or threaten to take any action they do not intend to take because that is illegal.

Example of Violations

Threatening to garnish wages before suit is filed.
Threatening to seize all personal items/have them sold at public auction.
Telling you directly or indirectly that you will be put in jail.
Threatening any action they do not intend to take such as a lawsuit.
Threatening any action that is illegal and cannot be taken.

807 Text. The following conduct is a violation. "The false representation or implication that a sale, referral, or other transfer of any interest in a debt shall cause you to (A) lose any claim or defense of payment of the debt; or (B) become subject to any practice prohibited by this title."

Explanation

They cannot imply that you will lose any claim or defense against the debt if the account is sold or transferred to someone else.

Example of Violations

Stating that they are going to give the account to someone else that is not covered under the F. D. C. P. A. for an extremely intense or strong-arm collection effort.

807 Text. The following conduct is a violation. "The false representation or implication that you committed any crime or other conduct in order to disgrace you."

Explanation

Cannot use false statements to instill fear or guilt in you.

Example of Violations

Claiming you committed fraud when there is no proof (their assumption is not sufficient). Claiming you are a criminal in any way. Indirect statements or insinuations that you or called party have committed fraud or a criminal act.

807 Text. The following conduct is a violation: "Communicating or threatening to communicate to any persons credit information which is known to be false, including the failure to communicate that a disputed debt is disputed."

Explanation

If a consumer's credit history is reported to a credit bureau, the information must be accurate, or advising the bureau that the account is disputed.

Example of Violations

Reporting any inaccurate or insufficient information to a credit bureau about you and/or failing to notify the bureau that the account is in dispute.

Example of Violations

Using simulated legal document format that makes you believe the account is in legal process. Using legal jargon in a letter that would give a false impression of the account status.

807 Text. This conduct is a violation. "The use of any false representation or deceptive means to collect any debt/to obtain information concerning a consumer."

Explanation

They cannot use false or deceptive means when attempting to locate a consumer or when collecting a debt.

Example of Violations

- Saying they are a friend of yours.
- Saying they have something of value for you.
- Using any other company name or affiliation.
- Saying you will have to "tell it to the judge."
- Giving a date that legal action will be taken and no legal action is then taken.
- Any false statements to locate you.
- $\sum$ Any false misrepresentations to locate you.
- Any false misrepresentation to coerce payment of a debt.

807 Text. The following conduct is a violation. "Except as otherwise provided for communications to acquire location information under Section 804, the failure to disclose clearly in all communications made to collect a debt or to obtain information about a consumer, that the debt collector is attempting to collect a debt and that any information obtained will be used for that purpose."

Explanation

When communicating with you, it must be absolutely clear that they are calling in an attempt to collect a debt and that any information obtained will be used for that purpose.

Example of Violations

Concealing the purpose of the call when speaking to you or responsible party.

807 Text. The following conduct is a violation. "The false representation or implication that accounts have been turned over to innocent purchasers for value."

Explanation

No false claims about the status of the debt are allowed.

Example of Violations

Claiming we now own the account and that you owe their company.

807 Text. The following conduct is a violation. "The false representation or implications that documents are a legal process."

Explanation

Stating or making insinuations that the suit is being or has been filed.

Example of Violations

Saying you will be in court next Tuesday, when they know this is a false statement. Using legal jargon to make you think suit is being filed or has been filed (in letters and/or conversations). Claiming that your wages will be garnished (before a judgment has been rendered).

807 Text. The following conduct is a violation. "The uses of any business, company, or organization name other than the true name of the debt collector's business, company, or organization."

Explanation

They cannot use any name other than the alias assigned to them or their real name. They must use only the true company name or its subsidiaries.

Example of Violations

Use of any other name than the true company name.

Using multiple alias names and not disclosing what company they are with.

807 Text. The following conduct is a violation. "The false representation or implication that documents are not legal and does not require action."

Explanation

If the account is in process, they should not say or imply that it is not.

Example of Violations

Telling you to disregard a court notice.
Telling a consumer that a suit has not been filed when, in actuality, it has been.

807 Text. The following conduct is a violation. "The false representation or implication that a debt collector operates or is employed by a consumer reporting agency as defined by law."

Explanation

They cannot inform you that they are a credit bureau.

Example of Violations

See the Explanation above.

SECTION 808 UNFAIR PRACTICE

808 Text. "A debt collector may not use unfair or unconscionable means to collect or attempt to collect any debt. Without limiting the general application of the foregoing, this conduct is a violation of this section:"

(808) Text. The following conduct is a violation. "The collection of any amount (including any interest, fee charge, or expense incidental to the principal obligation) unless such amount is expressly authorized by the agreement creating the debt or permitted by law."

Example of Violations

Adding an amount to the debt not in the original contract.

808 Text.   (The following conduct is a violation:)
"The acceptance by a debt collector from any person of a check or other payment instrument postdated by more than five days unless such person is notified in writing of the debt collector's intent to deposit such check or instrument not more than ten or less than three business days prior to such deposit."

"The solicitation by a debt collector of any postdated check or other postdated payment instrument for the purpose of threatening or instituting criminal prosecution."

Depositing or threatening to deposit any postdate check or other postdated payment instrument prior to the date on such check or instrument.

Explanation

If a check is postdated more than five days in advance, a notice must be sent at least three business days, but not more than ten, before depositing the check. They cannot solicit a check with intent to threaten or insinuate criminal prosecution.

Example of Violations

Telling you if the check is no good and that you risk going to jail. Telling you that they will prosecute. Failing to send a notice of intent to deposit the check at least three business days before, but not more than ten .

808 Text. The following conduct is a violation. "Causing charges to be made to any person for communications by concealment of the true purpose of the communication. Such charges include, but are not limited to, collect telephone calls and telegram fees."

808 Text. The following conduct is a violation. "Taking or threatening to take any non judicial action to effect dispossession or disablement of property if."

(A) There is no present right to possession of the property claim as collateral through an enforceable security interest;
(B) There is no present intention to take possession of the property; or
(C) The property is exempt by law from such dispossession/ disablement.

Explanation

A collector cannot take or threaten to take anything belonging to you which is not allowable by law.

Example of Violations

Threatening to take property through legal action that is exempt under law.

Threatening to seize property/personal possessions to sell them at auction.

Using false threats to scare you into paying.

808 Text. The following conduct is a violation: "Communication regarding a debt by post card."

Explanation

Post cards may not be used in collection of debts.

Example of Violations

Sending an open-faced collection notice.

808 Text. The following conduct is a violation. "Using any language or symbol, other than the debt collector's address, on any envelope when communicating with a consumer by use of the mails or by telegram, except that a debt collector may use his business name if such name does not indicate that he is in the debt collection business."

Explanation

They cannot use any designation on the outside of an envelope, which indicate that the contents concern a past due account/debt collection.

Example of Violations

Using the phrases "past due" or "collection division" on the outside of the envelope.

SECTION 809 VALIDATION OF DEBTS

809 (a) Text. "Within five days after the initial communication with a consumer in connection with the collection of any debt, a debt collector shall, unless the following information is contained in the initial communication or you have paid the debt, send you a written notice containing the amount of the debt, the name of the creditor to whom the debt is owed, a statement that unless you within thirty days after receipt of the notice, dispute the validity of the debt, or any portion thereof, the debt will be assumed to be valid by the debt collector; a statement that if you notify the debt collector in writing within the thirty-day period that the debt, or any portion thereof, is disputed.

The debt collector will obtain certification of the debt or a copy of a judgment against you and a copy of such verification or judgment will be mailed to you by the debt collector; and a statement that upon your written request within the thirty-day period, the debt collector will provide you with the name and address of the original creditor, if different.

Explanation

Within five days of the initial communication, a notice must be sent to give you the right to dispute and determine validity.

809 (b) Text. "If you notify the debt collector in writing within the thirty-day period described in subsection (a) that the debt, or any portion thereof, is disputed, or that you request the name and address of the original creditor, the debt collector shall cease collection of the debt, or any disputed portion thereof, until the debt collector obtains

verification of the debt or a copy of a judgment, or the name and address of the original creditor, and a copy of such verification or judgment, or name and address of the original creditor is mailed to you by the debt collector."

Explanation

Upon receipt of a written notice of dispute, they must cease communication with you regarding any disputed amounts until they are able to provide proof.

Example of Violations

Continuing to pursue a disputed amount of an account after written notification of the dispute has been received.

809 (c) Text. "The failure of a consumer to dispute the validity of a debt under this section may not be construed by any court as an admission of liability by you."

Explanation

If you fail to notify a debt collector of the dispute, it is not an admission of liability.

Example of Violations

Telling a consumer it is too late to dispute the account.

SECTION 816 RELATION TO STATE LAWS

816 Text. "This title does not annul, alter, affect, or exempt any person subject to the provisions of this title from complying with the laws of any state with respect to debt collection practices, except to the extent that those laws are inconsistent with any provision of this title, and then only to the extent of the inconsistency. For purpose of

this section, a state law is not inconsistent with this title if the protection such law affords any consumer is greater than the protection provided by this title."

FINALLY...We typically view bill collectors as the enemy, but if we learn how to "play the game," we can be the ultimate winners. This compilation of information was designed to give you facts that have not been readily disclosed before.

This chapter has provided you with the clearest explanation of the Fair Debt Collection Practices Act compiled. In summary, this chapter has addressed the following:

Harassment by third party debt collectors, credit grantors, in an effort to collect money owed to them. In most cases credit bureaus do not receive their information from these third party collection agencies, but from the credit grantor.

The following list outlines what a debt collector cannot do in collecting a debt for others:

* Contact you at inconvenient or unusual times unless you agree.

* Contact you at work against your employer's wishes.

* Contact you after you send written notice ("Drop Dead Letter") to an agency to stop, except to notify you that there will be no further contact other than by an attorney. At this time, they may not say that they will take legal action unless the creditor intends to do so, and has legal right to do so.

* Fail to give you written notice (within five days after contacting you), fail to tell you the amount owed, or the name of the creditor, and what to do if you feel you do not owe the money.

* Contact you about the debt if you deny owing the debt within 30 days after being contacted, unless you are sent proof of the debt.

* Make you pay for communications regarding such issues.

* Contact anyone but your attorney about your financial situation. [A third party collector may contact other people only to determine where you work or live.]

* Give false credit information about you to anyone.

* Advertise or publish your debt. Contact you by postcard that could advertise your debt.

* Put anything on an envelope (i.e. return address) that shows the communication is about the collection of a debt.

* Harass, oppress, or abuse any person, such as use of threats of violence or harm to property or reputation, use of obscene or profane language, or ongoing harassing or anonymous calls.

* Make false statements when collecting a debt, such as falsely imply that they are an attorney or government representative, use any false name, falsely imply that you have committed a crime or will be arrested for nonpayment, falsely imply that they work for a credit bureau, misrepresent the amount of debt, indicate papers are legal or "official"when they are not.

* Deposit a postdated check before the date of the check.

* Fail to apply amounts to the specific debts you choose.

A creditor may not threaten your credit rating while you're resolving a billing dispute. Once you have written about a possible error, a creditor must not give out information to other creditors or credit bureaus that would hurt your credit reputation. Until your complaint is answered, the creditor also may not take any action to collect the disputed amount.

After the creditor has explained the bill, if you do not pay in the time allowed, you may be reported as delinquent on the amount in dispute and the creditor may take action to collect. Even so, you can still disagree in writing. Then the creditor must report that you have challenged your bill and give you the name and address of each person who has received information about your account.

When the matter is settled, the creditor must report the outcome to each person who has received information. Remember that you may also place your own side of the story in your credit record (e.g. 100 - word statement).

As a consumer protected under the federal Fair Credit Reporting Act, you have the right to challenge or sue any credit-reporting agency if they fail to correct errors in your credit file or allow illegitimate access to your file.

You should also be aware that you can seek damages against any unauthorized person who accesses your credit report, or against any employee of a credit reporting agency who supplies a credit report to an unauthorized person.

BILL COLLECTORS
HAVE ONLY THE POWER THAT
YOU GIVE UP...

Rob Wilson

CHAPTER TEN

WAGE GARNISHMENT
LAW SUITS

In order for your wages to be garnished, a lawsuit must be filed. Once a judgment is enter by the courts a fifa is issued. The fifa will allow your creditor or the person who sued you to attach your employment or your bank account.

Like dealing with foreclosures, I feel strongly that it should not happen. If you are sued, you have thirty days to answer the lawsuit. Answering the lawsuit may prevent a judgment from going against you. By not answering the suit, a default judgment will be entered. This gives the upper hand to your creditor.

Unlike dealing with student loans, which have the authority to attach your wages directly, they have what is called an administration wage assignment. They can and will take 10% of your income.

Always, try to deal with your creditor before it gets to this point. That is the reason we put this information in the back. You have many options before it get to this point. What can you do if it does happen?

Never file bankruptcy just to stop the garnishment. If it is too late to stop the garnishment, I have two favorite ways of doing dealing with it. Offer a settlement of the amount to the creditor. Many times they will play hardball with you. By now, you should know the rules of the game.

Settlement is fast money to them that helps to give you an edge. Most likely the first person may not be the best to negotiate with. Use sound judgment, it is your best weapon.

My second choice is giving you some inside information. It's not top secret, it's information that most people do not know. You can offer a reasonable wage garnishment reduction. This reduction can both satisfy your creditor and even yourself.

Keeping mind, they are playing hardball because you made a bad decision not to work/deal with them. It is done all of the time. Let me point out that this is not law counseling. This is knowledge you should know, knowledge you can receive at your library. In Chapter twelve, you will find garnishment reduction letter that have worked very well. Please use them.

You must deal with the lawsuits. Dealing with one requires you to file an answer to the suit. This answer must state your argument. Be very careful of what you admit too. If an answer is not filed, as we stated earlier judgment by default is entered.

Once you file your answer, be very careful if you have any contact with the attorney. I have a great amount of respect for most attorneys, but the ones that deal with collection I personally do not trust.

Sometimes they will try to setup an arrangement to pay the debt off. Even before you file your answer. Any documents that they may offer you, can come back and hurt you. Most documents will be a consent judgment, there are times they may do a consent order. The difference between the two is the consent judgment will allow them the right to seek a garnishment if you do not keep the arrangement. The consent order is just the opposite. They will have to start the process over if you do not keep the arrangement.

If there is a default judgment against you, the best defense is a **motion to vacate and set aside.** This will allow you the chance to ask the court to hear your side of the case. Be sure to ask for a oral hearing. The attorney may request a summary judgment to be made. The summary judgment would be based on what you have admitted to.

Who is Covered?

Title III of the Consumer Credit Protection Act (CCPA) **protects employees from being discharged by their employers because of garnishment for any one indebtedness** and limits the amount of employees' earnings, which may be garnished in any one week.

Title III applies to all individuals who receive personal earnings and to their employers. Personal earnings include wages, salaries, commissions, bonuses and income from a pension or retirement program but do not ordinarily include tips. The law applies in all 50 states, the District of Columbia, Puerto Rico and all U.S. territories and possessions.

Basic Provisions/Requirements

Wage garnishment is a legal procedure through which the earnings of an individual are required by court order to be withheld by an employer for the payment of a debt. Title III prohibits an employer from discharging an employee whose earnings have been subject to garnishment for any one debt, regardless of the number of levies made or proceedings brought to collect it. **It does not, however, protect an employee from discharge if the employee's earnings have been subject to garnishment for a second or subsequent debt(s).**

Title III also protects employees by limiting the amount of their earnings that may be garnished in any workweek or pay period to the lesser of 25 percent of disposable earnings or the amount by which disposable earnings are greater than 30 times the federal minimum hourly wage prescribed by section 6(a) of the Fair Labor Standards

Act of 1938. This limit applies regardless of the number of garnish-ment orders received by an employer. In court orders for child support or alimony, Title III allows up to 50 percent of an employee's disposable earnings to be garnished if the employee is supporting another spouse or child, and up to 60 percent for an employee who is not. An additional 5 percent may be garnished for support payments, which are more than 12 weeks in arrears.

"Disposable earnings" is the amount of employee earnings left after legally required deductions have been made for federal, state and local taxes, social security, unemployment insurance and state employee retirement systems. Other deductions, which are not, required by law, e.g., union dues, subtracted from gross earnings when calculating the amount of disposable earnings for garnishment purposes.

Title III specifies that garnishment restrictions do not apply to bankruptcy court orders and debts due for federal and state taxes. Nor does it affect voluntary wage assignments, i.e., situations in which workers voluntarily agree that their employers may turn over some specified amount of their earnings to a creditor or creditors.

Assistance Available

Title III is administered and enforced by the Employment Standards Administration's Wage and Hour Division. More detailed informa-tion, including copies of explanatory brochures and regulatory and interpretative materials, may be obtained by contacting their offices.

Penalties

Violations of Title III may result in the reinstatement of a discharged employee, with back pay, and the correction of improper garnishment amounts. Where violations cannot be resolved through informal means, court action may be initiated to restrain and remedy violations.

Employers who willfully violate the discharge provisions of the law may be prosecuted criminally and fined up to $1,000, or imprisoned for not more than one year, or both. If a state wage garnishment law differs from Title III, the law resulting in the smaller garnishment, or prohibiting the discharge of any employee because his or her earnings have been subject to garnishment for more than one indebtedness must be observed.

**DO NOT WAIT
UNTIL THEY ARE READY
TO TAKE YOUR MONEY
BEFORE YOU ARE
READY TO DO SOMETHING.**

Rob Wilson

CHAPTER ELEVEN

LETTERS TO USE

This section of information and the letters that serve as examples of how you can get results from the credit reporting agency as well as your creditor.

It is important that you realize that at no time do any of your creditors wish to remove information from your credit. With reluctance they will. You have to be honest and consistent with your statements. Some consumers have also challenged the credit reporting agencies with similar information. If the credit reporting agencies cannot verify the challenge within thirty-five days, they will remove this information from your credit report.

There will be times that your account will show information that is inaccurate, incomplete or information that cannot be verified. It also can contain or show accounts that have been paid, but there is a balance remaining. You will want to use these letters to change the way a creditor forms his/her opinion.

When you use the letters regarding the completeness of your file, the credit reporting agencies will conduct an investigation. It is always important that you offer or show proof of the dispute you may have.

Try to put yourself in the place of the person in the letter, this will help you to really understand our direction.

Centurion American Bank
Suite 0002
Chicago, IL 60679-0002

RE: Financial Hardship
Account # 3739-915896-41009

Dear Customer Service Representative:

This letter is an attempt to resolve a delinquent debt owed to **The Bank,** I am currently on a fixed income. Due to medical reason I am unable to meet my basic day-to-day needs. I do not own property, neither is there any possible means to borrow money. All attempts to borrow money have failed. It is vitally important that you close my account and stop all interest and late charges.

I am attempting to enter into a hardship repayment arrangement on this account. I am hoping to reach repayment agreements to avoid seeking protection under a bankruptcy. Your acceptance of a hardship arrangement will help me avoid taking such steps. It has been and will always be my intention to repay all of my creditors. Your assistance at this time will allow me the opportunity to recover. I realize that without a compromise of the finance and late charges this debt will continue to escalate.

Please close this account in order to stop the additional charges.

Enclosed please find a financial statement.

Sincerely,

FINANCIAL HARDSHIP

IN THE STATE COURT OF DEKALB COUNTY
STATE OF GEORGIA

Plaintiff,	*	
	*	
vs.	*	CIVIL ACTION FILE #
Defendant	*	

MOTION TO VACATE AND SET ASIDE JUDGMENT

COMES NOW THE DEFENDANT, _____, in the above-style case and files this motion to vacate and side aside judgment and to request an oral hearing, plaintiff Attorney enter into a consent order and fail to supply the courts proper notification. No answer was filed because we had enter into a consent order with Plaintiff Attorney.

This 14 day of December 1999.

_____

Name

RULE NISI

The within and foregoing motion, having been read and consider, is hereby allowed and ordered filed, subject to objection. Let the Plaintiff, show case before Judge _____ at_____ AM. in Room No. _____ on the _____ day of _____ why the motion should not be granted.

This _____ day of _____ 1999.

_____

JUDGE, STATE COURT OF DEKALB COUNTY

CERTIFICATE OF SERVICE

This certify that I have on this date served a copy of the within and forgoing Answer to the Complaint on behalf of _____ upon _____, and _____ attorney's for Plaintiff by depositing a copy of same in the United States mail in a properly addressed envelope with adequate postage thereon as follows:

This 14 day of December, 1999.

_____ _____

VACATE AND SET ASIDE

STATE COURT OF   COUNTY

STATE OF _____

Medical Center Inc.,   File # 99vg100e

        Plaintiff,   *

                              *

vs.   *

                              *

Defendant.   *

        Garnishee   *

CONSENT AGREEMENT TO DECREASE GARNISHMENT AMOUNT

NOW COMES the Plaintiff, Hospital through it's attorney of record and You, Defendant consent and agree that the garnishee, County - Department of Finance will withhold Two Hundred Dollars($200.00) per pay period in lieu of 25% of the Defendant salary. This is to start upon the filing of the executed agreement.

This _____ day of _____ 1999.

_____

Judge State Court County

Consent to by:

_____

        Attorney for Plaintiff

_____

        Defendant

DECREASE GARNISHMENT

RE: Subordinate Garnishment
File 99vg0100340

Dear Account Rep.,

This letter is an attempt to resolve a delinquent debt and to subordinate an active or a pending garnishment. Your office has been awarded a judgment as well as a fifa to garnish the wages of _____ referred to our organization under the employee assistance program. This program is designed to assist employees who may be experiencing difficulty in various areas, which will have a direct affect on their continuous employment.

We realize that you have demonstrated due diligence in pursuit of trying to resolve this outstanding debt without legal remedies. Also, we will be the first to say that our client in the past did not honor their obligation.

This office has currently provided the needed counseling in budgeting, and money management that will allow consistent payment to your organization. Therefore, we are hoping to establish an arrangement to repay this debt without the instatement of the garnishment. Without your assistance at this time, my client is left with only three possible options:

Because of the garnishment, they may lose their employment or the garnishment will create financial hardship, which could result in bankruptcy.

I believe that we can resolve this matter, while at the same time protect the interest of your client. Once the employee assistance program gets involved, the stakes are very high for the employee. Please, help me protect your client as well as my own.

Sincerely,

STOP GARNISHMENT

October 17, 1996

General Federal C / U
Address
City, State

Dear Customer Service Representative :

For over the past 7 years my account with your bank has been a wonderful experience. Even though I had problems in the past, I did enjoy having the account when it was open.

The purpose of this letter is to attempt to gain some valuable information regarding my credit report. Currently, my credit report is showing that this account was charged off. It also shows my payments were made late on my account. That information is accurate, but it is now the only derogatory information that appears on my credit report.

The reason that those payments were made late is that I was a housewife and had just lost my husband it a violent death. As a single parent, I had no resources to maintain any credit. Since that time, I have maintained a job for two years and have satisfied all outstanding debt. As my record will indicate, that period was not consistent with my paying habit.

I am currently attempting to make a major purchase. My lender feels that the late payment will prevent him from underwriting the loan. Unless your organization will provide me and the credit reporting agencies a letter stating that these late payments should be removed immediately, this dream of mine will either be delayed or set aside.

Your help in this matter is greatly appreciated.

Sincerely,

CREDIT RATING CHANGE

October 17,1996

Equifax Credit Inf.
P. O. Box 740256
Atlanta, Georgia. 30374

Dear Customer Service Representative :

Recently, I received a copy of my credit report, and I found these items
that I believe to be incorrect and in error. These items on my credit report
are extremely detrimental and inadequately reflect my credit.

MFC Finance Co. //// Acct# 6B432112345 //// Open Date 5/94
Southeast Texas //// Acct # 0101010101 //// Balance $238.00
Dept. of Justice //// Acct # 44444444 //// Balance $811.00
Home Deport / MBGA //// Acct# CG66666666666 //// Open Date 3/94

By the provisions of 15 USC Section 1681i of the Fair Credit Reporting
Act of 1970, I formally demand that you conduct an investigation and
delete the inadequate and detrimental items from my report.

Please send me names and addresses of individuals that you have
contacted so that I may follow up. Also send me a copy of my credit
report reflecting the results and changes made.

Sincerely,

CREDIT REPORT INVESTIGATION

Equifax Credit Information
P. O. Box 740256
Atlanta, Georgia. 30374

RE: Dispute

Dear Customer Service Representative :

Recently, I received a copy of my credit report and I found several items that I know to be incorrect or in error. These items on my credit report are extremely detrimental and inadequately reflect my credit. These items have been paid or were included in a bankruptcy.

Paid / Bankruptcy Accounts

Commercial Credit //// Account # 60209091452 //// Amount $4298.00
Fidelity Financial Serv. //// Account 5783-010446 //// Amount $1090.00
Bloomingdales //// Account 399399802 //// Amount $86.00
Rich's //// Account 000000085022 //// Amount $431.00

By the provisions of 15 USC Section 1681i of the Fair Credit Reporting Act of 1970, I formally demand that you conduct an investigation and delete the inadequate and detrimental items from my report.

Please send me names and addresses of individuals that you have contacted, so that I may follow up. Also, send me a copy of my credit report reflecting the results and changes made.

Sincerely,

CREDIT REPORT INVESTIGATION

October 20, 1996

Equifax Credit Inf.
P. O. Box 740256
Atlanta, Georgia 30374

RE: Consumer Statement

Dear Customer Service Rep.,

In 1994, I was a full time housewife when my husband, who at the time, worked for the Atlanta Police Department was killed in the line of duty. Due to his death, I was forced to return to work to support my one-year-old son. During that period, I had problems paying my rent.

Since I have been on this job for over two years and have recovered financially, I am able to pay off all outstanding debts, as well as purchase a new home and start a savings account for any future emergencies. If there is ever a need to review my credit, please consider the facts of my past situation and judge me by present standing with my new creditors.

Sincerely,

Name
P. O. Box 12344
Atlanta, Georgia. 30331
222-99-4444
DOB 00/00/57

CONSUMER STATEMENT

Equifax Credit Information
P. O. Box 740256
Atlanta, Georgia 30374

RE: Consumer Statement

In August '94, I was involved in a car accident that put me out of work for four months. Receiving only disability pay that was 1/3 of my income, I was unable to pay my bills. After the threat of a lawsuit, reluctantly I consulted with an attorney who advised me that Chapter 7 would be my only recourse. Before filing Chapter 7, I provided all of my creditors a letter of protection. As my record indicates, prior to the accident, all debts were paid on time. All creditors included in Chapter 7 have been paid in full.

Sincerely,

CONSUMER STATEMENT

July 30, 2002

American Express
P. O. Box 2907879
Ft. Lauderdale, FL

Acct.. # 3731-134871-13003 Balance: $20,001.65
Attn. Unit Manager,

As an effort to prevent avoid my client from seeking protection under bankruptcy, we are arranging with a family member to borrow funds to settle this account.

Mr. Hines is currently the only source of income at this time. A large portion of their income was lost due to family sickness. It has always been their intention to honor all of their obligations. Presently one of his creditors are pursuing them legally. Their steps of legal action only provide my client with two options; 1) protection under bankruptcy, 2) compromise of balances to settle accounts.

Family members have arranged for funds to be available immediately, in the amount of $11,218.00, within the next ten business days, if you agreed to accept this amount as a full and final settlement of the above referenced account, a cashier check will be issued immediately. However, because a family member provides the funds, we would hope to resolve this as soon as possible.

If we have not heard from you within the next 24 hours, we will assume you have declined our offer. At which time, we will kindly notify you of the bankruptcy information that you would have preferred.

Sincerely,

SETTLEMENT LETTER

Address
City, State, Zip Code
Account #:
Balance: $

Dear Customer Service Representative :

This letter is an attempt to resolve a charged off or delinquent debt that has been or will be paid. My credit report is reflecting negative information that affects my ability to borrow money now and in the future. I respectfully request that the late payments that you are showing be removed, as well as changing the rating from an R5 to an R0 rating.

P. S. Upon acceptance of my request please notify me in writing. I respectfully request a letter showing that the changes are to be made.

Sincerely,

SETTLEMENT OFFER LETTER

October 3,1996

Bank
P. O. Box 27182
Richmond, Va. 23270-0001
Acct.. #
Balance: $5892.17

Dear Customer Service Representative :

As an effort to avoid filing bankruptcy, I have made arrangements with a family member to borrow funds with which to settle this account as well as with my other creditors.

Within the next thirty days, if you agree to accept $3830.00 as a full and final settlement of the above referenced account, a cashiers check will be issued immediately payable to the order of Bank. However, this offer is contingent on all creditors accepting partial payment as a full and final settlement in accordance with the attached list of creditors.

The balances shown on the attached list of creditors are based on the amounts owed when we first proposed our settlement.

This offer is good until ten days after the first thirty (30) days have ended. If we have not heard from you on or before this deadline, we will assume you have declined our offer, at which time, we will kindly notify you of the bankruptcy information that you would have preferred.

Sincerely,

SETTLEMENT OFFER LETTER

Name
1234 Anywhere Trl. S. W.
Atlanta, Georgia. 30331

Proposed Settlement to Creditors

Creditors Names	Balances	Proposed Settlement
1) C Bank P. O. Box 182 Richmond, Va. 23270-0001 Acct. #	$5892.17	$3830.00
2) FNNB P. O. Box 045 Louisville. Ky. 40285-5045 Acct. #	$587.10	$382.00
3) MBNA America P. O. Box 15137 Wilmington, De. 19886-5409 Acct. #	$3430.00	$2230.00
4) Sears P. O. Box 105702 Atlanta, Ga. 30348 Acct. #	$1784.01	$1160.00
5) National City Bank P. O. Box 85900 Louisville, Ky. 40285 Acct.. #	$440.75	$287.00
TOTALS	$12,134.03	$7889.00

SETTLEMENT OFFER LETTER

October 17,1996

National Control
46177 Warm Blvd.
Freemont, Ca. 94555
Account #: CS1B100425
Balance: $591.00

Dear Customer Service Representative :

This letter is an attempt to resolve a charged off or delinquent debt owed to Wards Dept. Store. Because my credit report is reflecting negative information that affects my ability to borrow money. I am willing to make an offer to settle the above account. My offer is $384.00 to settle in full the above debt. This offer is only good for the next 14 days. Upon your acceptance, I will forward you a cashier's check in that amount.

P. S. Upon your acceptance please notify me in writing. Also, upon receipt of my final payment, I respectfully request a letter showing that the account has a zero balance.

Sincerely,

SETTLEMENT OFFER LETTER

South Credit
P. O. Box 11113
Jonesboro, Georgia. 32237
Account # 55656
Regency

RE: Payment Arrangement

Dear Collection Rep.,

In compliance with the Fair Debt Collection Practice Act, you are required to honor the dates on check # 3351-check # 3356 in the amount of $20.00. These checks represent the monthly payment that I will be making over the next six months. I do not expect you to contact me any further by telephone. The F.D.C.P.A. entitles me to receive a notice from you that my checks will deposited on such date.

P. S. Any violations of this law entitle me to damages by your company.

Sincerely,

POST DATE TO THIRD ONLY

Receivable Corporate, Inc.
9 N. 95th Way, Suite 208
Scotland, AZ. 85258

Dear ,

Unfortunately, we were not able to communicate over the phone, therefore I have taken the necessary steps to deal with this outstanding debt. I am currently going through a separation and I am unable to pay this account. It is hard meeting my basic living expenses, without the ability to borrow money. Your request for the balance, a down payment or a settlement at this time is not possible. My intention is to sacrifice and make the best possible monthly payments that I can afford until such time I am able to reach a settlement agreement.

In compliance with the Fair Debt Collection Practice Act, you are required to honor the dates on check # 620 - check # 625 in the amount of $20.00. These checks represent the monthly payment that I will be making over the next six months. I do not expect you to contact me any further by telephone. The F.D.C.P.A. entitles me to receive a notice from you that my checks will deposited on such date.

You may forward any written communication to the above address. Any telephone communication shall be directed to our financial consultants Robert Wilson, at 555-555-5555. Your organization may receive calls to follow up on this account from Mr. Wilson. Your cooperation would be appreciated.

PS: Any violation of the F.D.C.P.A. entitles me to damages by your company.

Sincerely,

FORCED POST DATES TO THIRD PARTY ONLY

**THIS IS WHERE YOU SHOULD
NOW TAKE A DEEP BREATH.
IT WILL NOT BE THE SAME
FROM HERE ON...**

Rob Wilson

CHAPTER TWELVE

YOUR WEALTH IS YOUR POWER

I believe, that if you have read from the beginning, you will clearly understand this chapter. If you have skipped around, this chapter may not give you the fulfillment you desire.

Now, lets look back at what we have established about wealth. In chapter one, the spiritual laws of wealth was made clear in my mind. *But they that will be rich fall into temptation and a snare, and into many foolish and hurtful lust, which drown men in destruction and perdition.*

Understanding the spiritual laws of money, it has a distinct way of looking at riches and wealth. Many times when the word rich or riches is used, there seems to be a path to destruction. We end up chasing the material things that money can buy. We desire riches to enhance our status among friends and family.

This relates to the various styles that we talked about in Chapter Two. The way that we establish our relationship with money, determines how we show our pride.

There are many books that could be written on wealth alone. Because wealth in the minds of many is looked upon as how much money you have. The rich and famous are not called wealthy in most circles.

Why? Because money alone does not make you wealthy. The source of wealth I'm describing comes from the spiritual laws of money.

How can we justify our attempt to build wealth without the source? We want our own business, we play lotto, we save our money, and make investments in the stock market. But yet, we do not consider the source.

Deut. 8:17-18 And thou say in thine heart, my power and the might of my hand have gotten me this wealth. But thou shall remember the Lord thy God: for it is he that giveth the power to get wealth, that he may establish his covenant which he sware unto thy fathers, as it is this day.

When we realize that our ability to obtain wealth or riches can soon diminish, we then are able to understand that to maintain it, the principles of spiritual laws will allow growth. There is no way that I can talk with you about building wealth without identifying the true foundation.

Your true desire to build wealth may focus on many different things. The needs of your family, the pressure of society, and personal needs. It is the foundation that will stabilize you in the process. What you accept as your own standards, enable you to build from the bottom up.

I have colleagues that offer wealth in many different ways. Some offer it as MLMs, home base businesses, networking clubs, and investment clubs. Not that these things cannot create revenue, they very well can. I'm hoping that you are focusing on the foundation. Without the foundation, these will not work for you very well.

How many people do you know that have tried the let's get paid attitude. Are they now rich or wealthy today? It was intended from the beginning, that we prosper, and the prosperity has not abandoned us. We have abandoned it by adopting the system of this society as the foundation.

My challenge for you is that you except your original birth right. Return to spiritual laws as you deal in money, business, family, and in your church. You may be very surprised of the results you will receive.

The abundance of valuables is the primary concept that most people have about wealth. All of your personal goods such as cars, boats, jewelry, personal property, we discussed in a different way. We called them financial liabilities or assets, a part of your net worth not wealth.

The roots of wealth will be the principles we talked about all throughout the book. Your wealth is already present with you. If the theory of income producing assets is the source of wealth, then what is your primary number one asset? It is your own ability the earn an income.

If you do not maintain your lifestyle, or have control of your personal finances, your ability to create wealth will dissolve. Many people have received wealth in the form of lotto's, inheritance, gifts, and hard work. Yet we hear of stories everyday where they have fallen back further than they were.

If you took a person that is on welfare and gave them $100,000.00 in a lump sum, you find that they would mostly likely have spent all of this money within six months. Now, do not think that I have singled people on welfare out, I am not. Take the average working class and give them the same amount. It may take them just a little long to spend it.

The reason for this is simple. It is what we have been talking about all along. We do not understand the foundation of dealing with money. I have stated that your wealth is within you. You may ask, "Okay where is it?" I want you to be totally honest with yourself.

Consider these programs and answer the questions:

401k - Are you participating in the program? _____

Do you make the maximum contribution? _____
Are you borrowing from this program?_____

Do you know who is managing your 401 program? _____

Now, put these very same question towards retirement plans, IRA's, 403b, and pension or any compensation package.

Are you participating in these types of programs? If so, are you maximizing the amount that you can contribute? These programs can help you develop security, and create wealth.

To the contrary, if you are borrowing from these programs or do not know who is responsible for managing your programs, then you are losing all of your hope of security. These are some of the basic things that affect your ability to build wealth. Answer this questions. How different do you think your action would be with stocks and bonds?

Even if you are in these programs and participating, you still must understand that you will have to use sound judgment. Judgment is another source that must be used in every way when dealing with money.

Over confidence, is a killer to your finances when you are operating with misinformation. Every source of information cannot apply to your situation. Having unwarranted confidence in your decision-making, and judgment leads to other problems as well.

The over confidence creates a need to compete that really takes us off of the primary goals that we may set. Just hours ago, I was speaking with a lady who lives in an apartment complex. I asked her why not live in a house? She stated that she wanted one, but she is waiting to get her credit in shape. Her claim to get her credit in shape was due to competing with a family member in purchasing household items. In the process, she over extended herself with credit card debt. Now she has to face this battle alone. Regardless who has the best looking home. It's still an apartment.

Earlier, we talked about your relationship with money. People can get very emotional with and about money that any proper decision made can be disastrous. I would hope that this book has helped you to identify your emotional reaction to financial situations. This is so personal. Your approach, your determination, and the decision to make sound judgment is key.

Mortgage Reduction Theory

Mortgages can cost you a lot of money, even though it is a great investment. Remember, we spoke about this being the single largest investment you may possibly have in your lifetime. Many times consumers panic at the closing table when they see what the total cost of the home will be over thirty years.

Consider this, if you purchased a home value at $100,000.00 and the interest rate is 7.5% for thirty years, your mortgage payment will be around $699.00 per month. If you included your property taxes of $1000.00 a year and hazard insurance $300.00 a year. Your total mortgage payment will be around $807.00 a month. This is not the reason they panic. The reason they panic is the total cost of the mortgage after amortization for 360 months. At the above interest rate of 7.5% on a $100.000.00 home, the total cost is $251,721.99. You would pay over $151,000.00 in interest alone.

Now, should you panic? No, there are some basic ways that you can reduce your mortgage. You can control the total amount of money paid to your mortgage company. The downside to this is that you will not maintain what is needed to really get the best results.

When you think about it, over recent years you have been told to make extra payments to pay off your mortgage earlier. This will reduce your mortgage down to as low as fifteen years. In addition, there are the bi-weekly payments that you can make that will range from twenty-two to sixteen years.

Now, if this was so easy I have only one question. Why is everybody not doing it?

The fact is simply this, without the consistency of maintaining the extra or bi-weekly payment you really will not make a difference. Your extra payment needs to be made each month towards the mortgage. Just missing one single extra payment can wipe out at least four of the previous that you would have gained.

This is why they created that escrow account, which would allow you to save $30,000.00 after thirty years. The question you should ask is, why are they willing to tease me with $30,000.00, is it possible that I can save more? Look at it this way, if you paid your mortgage bi-weekly, you will have saved $40,101.22. In essence, what you are really doing is adding a 13th payment to your annual number of payments, and splitting it up between 26 bi-weekly payments. Which means that by coughing up an extra $26.89 every two weeks you will pay off your mortgage in 279 months instead of the current 361 months, and save $40,101.22 in mortgage interest in the process.

On the next page is the actual amortization table for the mortgage we are discussing. This information shows you the principle and interest payments. It is amazing how much you can pay towards your mortgage each year, and then look at what really went towards your principle balance. It can become very disturbing when you really look at an amortization table, and identify what little damage you are really doing yearly.

Compound interest is compounding against you in this case. As you review the table on the next page, notice the process and learn it. Later in the book, you will see another form of compound interest that you can have working for you. This table is not taking into account your property taxes and insurance. You will need to factor those numbers at a later time. The focus is on principle and interest annually.

Principal Amount of Loan: $ 100,000.00
Annual Interest Rate: 7.50   **Term of the loan in years:** 30.00
Start with month: May   **Start with year:** 2000

Monthly payment will be $ 699.21

Totals in the year 2000 – 2001

Month	Principal	Interest	Balance
May	74.21	625.00	99925.79
June	74.68	624.54	99851.11
July	75.14	624.07	99775.96
August	75.61	623.60	99700.35
September	76.09	623.13	99624.26
October	76.56	622.65	99547.70
November	77.04	622.17	99470.66
December	77.52	621.69	99393.14
January	78.01	621.21	99315.13
February	78.49	620.72	99236.63
March	78.99	620.23	99157.65
April	79.48	619.74	99078.17

Totals in the year 2000 – 2030

Year	Prin.	Interest	Balance	Year	Prin.	Interest	Balance
2000	606.86	4986.85	99393.14	2016	2974.12	5416.45	70589.94
2001	968.94	7421.63	98424.19	2017	3205.01	5185.56	67384.93
2002	1044.16	7346.41	97380.03	2018	3453.82	4936.75	63931.11
2003	1125.22	7265.35	96254.81	2019	3721.95	4668.62	60209.16
2004	1212.58	7177.99	95042.23	2020	4010.90	4379.67	56198.26
2005	1306.71	7083.85	93735.51	2021	4322.27	4068.30	51875.99
2006	1408.16	6982.41	92327.36	2022	4657.82	3732.75	47218.17
2007	1517.48	6873.09	90809.88	2023	5019.42	3371.15	42198.75
2008	1635.28	6755.29	89174.60	2024	5409.09	2981.48	36789.66
2009	1762.23	6628.34	87412.36	2025	5829.01	2561.56	30960.64
2010	1899.04	6491.53	85513.32	2026	6281.53	2109.04	24679.11
2011	2046.47	6344.10	83466.86	2027	6769.19	1621.38	17909.93
2012	2205.34	6185.23	81261.52	2028	7294.70	1095.87	10615.23
2013	2376.55	6014.02	78884.97	2029	7861.00	529.57	2754.23
2014	2561.04	5829.52	76323.92	2030	2754.23	43.18	0.00

Now, I personally recommend that you consider a bi-weekly repayment plan that I will talk about more. Nevertheless, you must also be very careful with whom you do the program. There are a number of programs you know of that may not be for you and your household. The whole purpose of this book is to release your financial power.

There are programs that I think get more credit than they deserve. Therefore, right now I am going to give you my opinion of some of them. Remember, knowledge can be power when it is used properly.

One of my pleasures is giving financial seminars. In the seminars, I see the amazement on the faces of the audience when I share with them the fact that I do not like 20, 15, or ten-year mortgages. I believe that it is creating financial hardship on the consumer. I know that a lot of financial consultants feel very good about them, I do not.

I believe that my reasoning is very clear. Let me talk about it for a moment. If you can afford to make the payments on a 20, 15, or ten year mortgage. Why? When you obligate yourself to such a payment, you can really set yourself up for financial hardship. What happens if you have an unforeseen financial emergency? The higher payment obligation can put you in a situation that will prevent you from paying your mortgage on time.

Most new homeowners have the passion to really go after their mortgage in the first year. Moreover, with all of the best intentions they end up finding themselves in a foreclosure position in a short period. After working with people in such a position, I found that most foreclosures happen within the first five years of home ownership. Many people feel that if they can shorten the number of years to be obligated that it is a great accomplishment. It is after the fact they realize that they are in trouble.

Later in this section, you will see that whatever a 20, 15, or ten year mortgage can offer with the higher payment, the same if not better results can be obtained for much less. That is why I hate those trap setting mortgage terms.

In addition, you have the principle payment type. This type of mortgage offers you the chance to make one additional payment each year and reduce the number of years from thirty to twenty-three years. As you can see, it sounds good also. Again, there is nothing wrong with reducing your mortgage down in this matter except that there is a simpler way to do it with greater results.

The bi-weekly plan, allows you to divide or split your monthly payment in half. This method allows you to make twenty-six payments in twelve months. It also will reduce your mortgage from thirty years to about nineteen years. Very similar to the principle payment mortgage, you are making thirteen payments in twelve months. Some will make additional principle payments every now and then. It may save seven years off of a thirty-year mortgage.

Listen, any mortgage reduction is always good, but what happens when you could have more reduction for less money? I guess I made my point that I do not like them. So, allow me to share with you what I think would really make your eyes light up. How about a thirteen or nine year mortgage. Get more reduction for less.

I believe that when we look at our finances and determine that we can afford a higher payment, it does not mean that we have to obligate ourselves to it. For my purposes, I want to show you some of the plans that I am familiar with and have knowledge of. Now, I'm sure that there are others that you know about. Nevertheless, I will only use the following.

Often times I talk about thing that really provide you with options. Mortgage reduction to me is not an option; it is mandatory. It is the single highest investment that you will ever make. Any attempt to gain wealth should begin with eliminating this liability.

Consider if you mortgage company can offer you a reduction plan from thirty years to twenty-two years, or reducing it from twenty-two years to nineteen years or fifteen years. Would you think that they could give you a plan to reduce your mortgage down to nine or less years? There is currently no watchdog for mortgage companies and no monitoring system when you receive an amortize payment schedule. In many cases, consumers can pay an average of $15,000-$20,000 more than they should.

Did you know that on any day of the week you could pay the principle balance of your mortgage without penalty? With the exception of most second mortgages, there should not be a pre-payment penalty. Often times consumers try to reduce the total cost of their mortgage in many different ways. Some try balloon notes, twenty year, fifteen year, and ten years mortgages and really have not saved what they should.

This is one of the most profitable businesses next to credit cards. When you consider that over the next thirty years you will pay more than 150% of your mortgage. So, when they offer you the opportunity to reduce it to twenty-two years and save $40,000.00 it sounds like a big deal right? Basically, what they did was reduce their profit by about 17%. On a home valued at $100,000.00 it will cost you over $240,000.00. Now consider the interest rate is 7.50% and the monthly payment is $699.21. If your mortgage company reduced your mortgage from thirty to twenty-two years, it will now cost you $199,974.06.

If you are not sure how I came up with these numbers, take a look. If being on a biweekly payment program reduces your mortgage to twenty-two years you are making the equivalent of thirteen payments in twelve months. Multiply $699.21 by 13 months and then multiply that total by 22 years.

What happens when you take a thirty-year mortgage and go on a biweekly prepayment program and add a principle payment? It is my belief, that when you have established a prepayment arrangement and attack it consistently, you reduce the amount of interest that you pay by a far greater number than 17%. Now, on the next three pages we can see the difference in what you can have in 18 months on a biweekly plan, a normal thirty-year, and a fifteen year plan. Remember I believe that getting more for less is much better. Also, notice that the fifteen-year mortgage payment is over three hundred dollars more.

Biweekly Mortgage- 15.33 years

Starting with $100000 at 7.50 % Payment of $ 699.21 plus $150.00.
Biweekly means two extra principal payments a year of $ 424.61

Month	(Year)	Balance	Payment	Interest	Paid Principal
1	0.08	99775.79	849.21	625.00	224.21
2	0.17	99550.18	849.21	623.60	225.61
3	0.25	99323.16	849.21	622.19	227.02
4	0.33	99094.72	849.21	620.77	228.44
5	0.42	98864.85	849.21	619.34	229.87
6	0.50	98633.54	849.21	617.91	231.30
BW	-	98208.94	424.61		424.61
7	0.58	97973.54	849.21	613.81	235.40
8	0.67	97736.66	849.21	612.33	236.88
9	0.75	97498.30	849.21	610.85	238.36
10	0.83	97258.46	849.21	609.36	239.85
11	0.92	97017.11	849.21	607.87	241.34
12	1.00	96774.26	849.21	606.36	242.85
BW	-	96349.66	424.61	-	424.61
13	1.08	96102.63	849.21	602.19	247.02
14	1.17	95854.06	849.21	600.64	248.57
15	1.25	95603.94	849.21	599.09	250.12
16	1.33	95352.25	849.21	597.52	251.69
17	1.42	95099.00	849.21	595.95	253.26
18*	1.50	94844.16	849.21	594.37	254.84
BW	-	94419.55	424.61	-	424.61
19	1.58	94160.46	849.21	590.12	259.09
20	1.67	93899.76	849.21	588.50	260.71
21	1.75	93637.42	849.21	586.87	262.34
22	1.83	93373.44	849.21	585.23	263.98
23	1.92	93107.82	849.21	583.58	265.63
24	2.00	92840.53	849.21	581.92	267.29
BW	-	92415.93	424.61	-	424.61
25	2.08	92144.32	849.21	577.60	271.61
26	2.17	91871.01	849.21	575.90	273.31
27	2.25	91595.99	849.21	574.19	275.02
28	2.33	91319.26	849.21	572.47	276.74
29	2.42	91040.79	849.21	570.75	278.46
30	2.50	90760.59	849.21	569.00	280.21

15-Year Mortgage

Amount Financed $100000   Interest Rate 7.5%
Number Of Payments 180   Monthly Payment $927.01

Payment Number	Balance Before	Payment Interest Paid	Principal Paid	Interest Paid To Date
1	100000.00	625.00	302.01	625.00
2	99697.99	623.11	303.90	1248.11
3	99394.09	621.21	305.80	1869.33
4	99088.30	619.30	307.71	2488.63
5	98780.59	617.38	309.63	3106.01
6	98470.96	615.44	311.57	3721.45
7	98159.39	613.50	313.51	4334.95
8	97845.88	611.54	315.47	4946.48
9	97530.40	609.57	317.44	5556.05
10	97212.96	607.58	319.43	6163.63
11	96893.53	605.58	321.43	6769.21
12	96572.10	603.58	323.43	7372.79
13	96248.67	601.55	325.46	7974.34
14	95923.21	599.52	327.49	8573.86
15	95595.72	597.47	329.54	9171.34
16	95266.19	595.41	331.60	9766.75
17	94934.59	593.34	333.67	10360.09
18*	94600.92	591.26	335.75	10951.35
19	94265.17	589.16	337.85	11540.50
20	93927.31	587.05	339.96	12127.55
21	93587.35	584.92	342.09	12712.47
22	93245.26	582.78	344.23	13295.25
23	92901.03	580.63	346.38	13875.89
24	92554.66	578.47	348.54	14454.35
25	92206.11	576.29	350.72	15030.64
26	91855.39	574.10	352.91	15604.74
27	91502.48	571.89	355.12	16176.63
28	91147.36	569.67	357.34	16746.30
29	90790.02	567.44	359.57	17313.74
30	90430.45	565.19	361.82	17878.93

30-Year Mortgage
Amount Financed $100000   Interest Rate 7.5%
Number Of Monthly Payments 360   Payment $699.21

Payment Number	Balance Before	Interest Paid	Principal Paid	Interest Paid Payment To Date
1	100000.00	625.00	74.21	625.00
2	99925.79	624.54	74.67	1249.54
3	99851.12	624.07	75.14	1873.61
4	99775.98	623.60	75.61	2497.21
5	99700.37	623.13	76.08	3120.33
6	99624.28	622.65	76.56	3742.98
7	99547.72	622.17	77.04	4365.16
8	99470.69	621.69	77.52	4986.85
9	99393.17	621.21	78.00	5608.06
10	99315.17	620.72	78.49	6228.78
11	99236.68	620.23	78.98	6849.01
12	99157.7	619.74	79.47	7468.74
13	99078.22	619.24	79.97	8087.98
14	98998.25	618.74	80.47	8706.72
15	98917.78	618.24	80.97	9324.96
16	98836.81	617.73	81.48	9942.69
17	98755.33	617.22	81.99	10559.91
18*	98673.34	616.71	82.50	11176.61
19	98590.83	616.19	83.02	11792.81
20	98507.82	615.67	83.54	12408.48
21	98424.28	615.15	84.06	13023.63
22	98340.22	614.63	84.58	13638.26
23	98255.64	614.10	85.11	14252.36
24	98170.53	613.57	85.64	14865.92
25	98084.88	613.03	86.18	15478.95
26	97998.70	612.49	86.72	16091.45
27	97911.99	611.95	87.26	16703.40
28	97824.73	611.40	87.81	17314.80
29	97736.92	610.86	88.35	17925.66
30	97648.57	610.30	88.91	18535.96

Now, I will begin to talk about what my theory is as it relates to paying off your mortgage earlier. But, first allow me to clarify what my purpose really is. To help you save money. Never before have I heard of a mortgage program that can provide you the results that I am about to discuss. I remember the night that a very dear friend of mine called me and gave me the results. She stated that my system on a $100,000.00 home at 7.5% with a monthly payment of $699.21 could be reduced to 9.4 years.

That was a moment of joy and also great disappointment for me. As she begin look at her brand new mortgage payment to find out her own results, she discovered and error. The error would not allow what we wanted to accomplish. Because of this error, we realized that the current methods of applying interest and principle payments would not give us the results we would like. Therefore, this is a theory that we hope will foster change in the banking and mortgage industry. I believe that in the months and years to come, you will find more and more banks having to convert the way they apply mortgage payments.

Today, you have to be very careful about what you do with money. There are so many different scams, so that when something good comes along you feel the need to question it. As I talk more about what my theory is and what it can do for you, I will also try to remove all the doubt that you may have. Remember, this may sound too good to be true.

As you have seen with the other mortgage tables, even though you saved money, it is no where near what you could have saved. The bank is still making a huge profit. I do not want to discourage anyone from using any program that you may utilize now. But, consider the fact that you can reduce your principle as often as you would like without being penalized as we discussed earlier.

To understand my theory, let me set the tables with some key facts regarding interest payments. The amount of interest applied to a mortgage balance is amortized is this manner. You would take the principle balance and multiply it by the interest rate and than divide it by the number of months on the contract to get the daily cost. **Example: $100,000.00 x 7.5% = $7,500 ÷ 360 = $20.83.**

Now, in order to get the monthly cost multiply $20.83 by the number of days in that month. **Example: $20.83 x 30 = $624.90.** This is the area where I want to begin looking. If you can reduce your principle whenever you would like, that means you should be able to change the principle balance. Changing your principle balance should change your interest payment.

If you ask any banker or loan officer how the interest is calculated you may be surprised that many of them do not know. But, we trust their judgment about our personal finances. If you look back at the fifteen-year mortgage schedule or any bi-weekly schedule you will find that the principle payments are made once or twice a year.

This mean, your principles balance only changes two additional times in that year. Therefore the amount of interest that could have been saved could be minimum. But, if you split those payments over twelve months to reduce the principle twelve additional times, your principle balance would actually change twenty-four times in twelve months. Not fourteen under the current method. I have asked bankers, "Why not post additional principle payments monthly? The question is never really answered.

Any mortgage reduction program is great, but as a consumer you will have to demand what you want. The only reason they can possibly give is that the computer makes the calculation. Your response should be, "who wrote the formulas, that your computer calculates?"

Let me end with my theory by asking you this question. If only two additional principle payments can reduce it to under sixteen years, what would happen if the principle payment was applied on twelve months?

You have the right to apply principle payment any time that you like. Do so as often as you can. Test your mortgage company just by sending a small payment towards the principle and see what would really happen. If you cannot notice the reduction of that payment, you would want to watch them closely. Also, watch out for negative amortization as well. There is so much involved with mortgages that I am currently working on a tape series on the subject.

PUTTING IT TOGETHER

Remember that there are many styles and ways for which you handle money. Use clear and consistent information to minimize and eliminate the fear you once had. Once you have examined your own styles of money management, then you can move forward to setting your budget. As you set the budget you must identify the things that have gotten you in trouble before.

Even though your process may appear to be complex and intimidating, you will have to use all of the principles in Chapter One to truly simplify the process. Your goal setting, along with your budget, will allow you the chance to get ahead. This is one of the things that I felt necessary to really talk about in this chapter. Looking ahead can really cover all of the areas that affect your life.

Your plans and goals should consist of short term and long term. If you are going to save, eliminate debt, and invest in insurance products, short and long term goals will be a great part of the plan. You must act, not just create the plan.

Once I wrote a business plan that actually worked it's way back to the beginning. I mean that I started at my preceded destination and worked all the way back to the starting point. The results of the business plan went very well. Surprisingly, I was able to identify most of the problems that I would have to confront.

Setting your goals may appear to be a challenge to you, so simply write down what it is that you would like to accomplish. Then take some time and really think about it. Once you have given yourself time to think about it, you may find that it really is not difficult.

Have a plan in place that will not change how you live. The idea of setting goals is not to decrease your standard of living but to enhance it. Look at the example on the next page.

Let's say that your goal is to save $5,000.00 in three years, while at the same time eliminate $5000.00 in credit card debt. For this scenario, we are consider the interest rate on the credit card debt is 16% and that you have $325.00 in discretionary income. Discretionary income is the amount of income remaining after all of your expenses are paid.

You will need to save $139.00 a month to reach the goal of $5,000.00 in three years. You should place your savings in a high interest bearing account. I really would recommend that you find something with compound interest. The interest on your credit card is normally compounded, now you can have compound work for you.

The normal life expectancy on the credit card balance of $5,000.00 with 16% interest is about 555 months, a little over 46 years. This is true if you are only making the minimum monthly payment, and there are no new charges. So, in order to reduce this debt in three years, it appears that you have your work cut out for you.

Not really. There is $186.00 remaining in your discretionary income. In addition to your normal minimum payment, you would send an extra $100.00 separately. By doing so consistently, you will decrease you principle balance monthly. This reduces the amount of interest that you would have had to pay. Now, you would have paid this off within the amount of time that you set out to do.

There were no changes in the home expenses, only the discretionary income eliminated the debt and created the results. Understanding what you are having to deal with is so important for the best results. Staying with your set goals allows you to really feel the accomplishment that you have made.

Unlike going on a diet, you are simply managing your money. I definitely believe that as you understand more about dealing with your finances, you will fell better about yourself. Do not begin to think that you are the only person that is going though things such as this.

Hopefully, you have learned the different styles of money management and mismanagement. It is important that you understand that the money mistakes you made in the past are not relevant at this point. But, if you return to your old principles of dealing with money, then wealth may not be your desire.

Most intelligent people with money make the very same mistakes you do. Nobody likes feeling stupid, so often times we fail to look at our situation, in fear of just that. I have counseled thousands of individuals and families and they all have felt to some degree inadequate. They all have bad, I mean bad spending habits. Having bad habits and no relationship with money is a very common problem.

To break that cycle is not easy no one has gotten into financial trouble overnight. Therefore, your efforts will take a little time. Like any relationship there are different stages. Each stage will take you to a different level, and each level provides you with greater results. Because we are talking about money, the plan that you use to set your goals will depend greatly on how the relationship is established.

This may not come as a surprise to you, but most people do not have a relationship with their money. When I do seminars, one of my favorite set up questions is, "How many of you can give me the actual amount of your last paycheck?" Less than 10% of the audience will actually know the amount of the last paycheck. Even though many others were close to their amount, it does not count. You cannot really feel good about that.

We talked earlier about your ability to earn an income as being your most valuable asset. Yet, most people do not know the meaning of income. Many people pay their bills on time each month. Without the relationship with the money, there is not a plan of action. Therefore, often times they end up living from paycheck to paycheck. They are not able to understand the principle, make sound judgment, set goals, and develop the relationship necessary to create wealth.

HOW DOES THE RELATIONSHIP WORK?

When I talk about the relationship with money, I am talking about the Jed Clampet syndrome. The Jed Clampet syndrome is having a complete relationship with your money and with your bank. Many people do not understand this simple point.

They say, that banks only lend money to people who do not need money. If you need money, you will not get it from the bank. That statement is true only when you operate with your money without the relationship. Banks are in the business to lend money. We have to be in business to receive the money. No relationship, no money.

Now, everybody remembers Jed Clampet. He was a hillbilly that became rich overnight. And immediately his very first new friend not only became his neighbor, but his banker as well. Mr. Clampet would just show up at the bank, walk right in the office and receive anything he wanted. His relationship went as far as his money took him. The relationship that I would like to make very clear to you is very simple. You will not create wealth without the relationship with the bank.

I hope you understand that you must use sound judgment with money. Like everything else, you have to build this relationship from the bottom up.

We talked about how to save money, now we will put money and relationship to work for you. If you are only able to save $20.00 a week, then put this money in a certificate of deposit(CD). As little as $20.00 a week is a $1000.00 a year. Using the products that a bank offers can be to your advantage. I chose a CD because there are banks that offer different programs with CD's. The one that I like the most will allow you to make small payments towards a larger amount and pay interest on your money. This does not sound like much now, just wait until you hear the whole story. You might finally change your mind about some things you felt about banks and CD's.

When you go into a bank to borrow money, there are thing you should know. The first is this, a loan officer is not just going to loan you money without feeling sure that it is a great chance that they will get their money back. He does not know you, but you expect him to give you a loan. So what you have had a checking account with this bank for ten years. That is all you had, a source to write a check. You do not even understand why he asked for your social security number. It is not just to run a credit report. It is a whole lot more.

The loan officer is trying to make his very first decision about giving you the money. So, he will want to look at your records at the bank to see what type of relationship you already have with them. Sadly to say, it is not only your checking account. He is looking for other products that you may have with the bank. Believe it or not, this is the bank's first consideration. Even with credit problems you can borrow money from the bank if the relationship is right.

Remember, we talked about assets, and what assets are. If not, look back in chapter two, we talk about your personal net worth and what the sources are. All bank applications asks you to provide them information in those areas. To keep your mind fresh of what they are, here is a partial list of them.

and checking acct.(s)	Mutual funds
gs account(s)	Corporate bonds
Money market funds	Municipal bonds
Life ins. cash values	Certificates of Deposit
U. S. savings bonds	IRA /other retirement plans
Brokerage accounts	Profit-sharing account
Common stocks	Thrift plan accounts

These areas can determine your ability to get the loan even before they look at your credit file. Also, in addition to this information, if they know you by name, you can be put ahead of the game. We are talking about relationships with money as well as the bank. What type of relationship do you have with your bank?

The products on the previous page normally are the very same items that you will find on the loan application. The way that you should be able to develop and build money in these areas should be clear. If not, the budget that you have set up should be your guide. With proper planning there will be money to save. As you save money, you should begin developing two or more of the products. By setting goals in this area, you move up a level as there is growth.

Most people will tell you that there is no money in CD's. Consider a family that has had credit problems in the past. Now they are on a budget and saving money. This family in the past, has never save a dime longer than three months. Their current budget allows their long term savings to be $167.00 a month, which will provide them $2004.00 a year. With this money placed in a CD, they can receive the current interest rate on a monthly basis. At the end of the twelve months, they will have ten days to decide what they would like to do with the deposit. I recommend that they roll it over for another year or lock it down for two or more years.

Locking the money down for two or more years can earn a higher interest rate on a compounding daily average. Money that has interest compounded daily is very good. It is also safe in the CD as well. On the other hand, if the money is rolled over, then you are building on top of what you already have. This allows you the ability to borrow against the money if there is an emergency.

Right now, the relationship that you may have with your bank is probably direct deposit. I would recommend that you go down to a local branch that is very convenient to you. This way it will be easy for you to drop by from time to time. Once you're at the bank sit down and get to know the loan officer. Be very clear about what you want to do at the bank. If you are not clear about what you want to do, please do not go to the bank. Save yourself the embarrassment. Unlike what most people think, bankers are no different than we are at forming an opinion of others.

You must be properly dressed. You would want to establish that your purpose it to develop a financial portfolio with his bank. Tell him that you will be able to deposit money on a regular basis. It must be clear that you are not there for a loan now or in the future. Your goal is to build for your financial future. In most cases, the loan officer is stunned and will be impressed about what they are hearing. Work this new relationship carefully, get on a first name basis, and get to know the bank tellers. Once you are at a point where they all know you on sight. You would never have to pull out identification again.

That is my favorite part about my bank, no identification is needed. How did I get to this point? It was not easy, it took a little time to plan my goals. It also took time to get to know all of the tellers also. That will also be very important for you.

This is how I did it. After meeting with the loan officer, he informed me that he would be glad to help me in this area. I developed a financial portfolio. After I had gotten a good review from him, I moved on to the tellers. Every other day I would go by the bank, some days I would make a deposit, and others I would just check my balance. It became a joke with the tellers. All I wanted to do was to check my balance. After a few weeks, they all knew me by name. I did not have a lot of money in the bank, but I had established a relationship.

I remember one Saturday morning I was out playing basketball and needed to make a deposit. When I ran into the bank there was a long line for the tellers and customer service. I immediately looked in the branch managers office. He saw me and called me in. He took my deposit to a teller and returned with my deposit slip. The people in line looked at me very funny. I'm sure they wondered who I was, or they may have thought that I had a lot of money. But, it was the relationship with the bank.

I had even invited the banker to speak at a seminar to validate his importance to me. He was honored to speak, and the relationship has blossomed everyday since.

Knowing a personal banker today can be very difficult, but, it is very possible. You must make it happen because they are there to serve you. With direct deposit, telephone banking, and banking on the internet there is no relationship. Your relationship with the bank ranks very high in the most important relationships to have. Consider the fact that most families have some type of relationship with finance companies. Finance companies borrow the money they lend to you from the bank. They have established a relationship to be the middleman for you.

The same is true when you buy a car. They search for a finance company to finance the car for you. I could go on and on about the many companies that act as a middleman to provide money to you. This is another reason why relationships are important. It costs you more when you use or go through a middle person to borrow money. Make this a personal issue for you and your family. Provide, protect, and preserve your family. It is a part of the foundation that we have been learning. Not establishing a solid relationship with the bank will make everything else that you do complicated. Isn't it funny how relationships can make a difference.

The relationship that you have with family, your coworkers, your church, your God, and your money determines the outcome. Many things that we perceive to be the right way, a biblical reference tells us that it is a way unto death. *Proverbs 14: 12 There is a way which seemeth right unto a man; but the end thereof are the ways of death. Death in our financial lives affects everything we do here on earth.* Most hard working everyday people work from paycheck to paycheck, and are just a paycheck away from being homeless. Many times they rely on the misinformation that they receive from friends. These friends have the best of intentions, but do not know that they themselves are relying on bad information.

For generations, we have never really been taught how to deal with money. We may have seen grandma put her money in a handkerchief. Then mom would always use a snuff can to hide her money, aunt Sue, well, she was a little more personal where she put her money. These are really the only relationships that most can identify with.

ELIMINATING YOUR LIABILITIES

Liabilities can cost you thousands of dollars over the life of repaying your obligations. Now, I am sure that you have come up with a lot of your own liabilities at this point. Some that you may not have realized were a liability. While we are concerned about the availability of cash, we often overlook the need to eliminate liabilities.

Sometimes the emphasis is on disposable income, not considering the amount of liability that is created. Even though, it is possible to have some disposable income and still be in a ruined financial state. The amount of liability that is create really affect any goals that you may have. There are liabilities that will allow you to turn them into cash, and there are liabilities that just eat out of your pocket. Just as you would have to plan a budget, you should plan to eliminate liability.

There is no way that I am aware of, that you can create wealth and liabilities at the same pace. Think of the number of athletes, musicians, and movie stars who are broke today. It is not for the lack of money, it is due to mismanagement of money. The choices they made in regards to accumulating large and unnecessary items which overwhelmed them with liability. With all of the money that they made, they ended up having to sell everything that they had. There are many lesson that you can learn without having to take the class. Yet, we chase after the very things we see others lose.

Earlier we talked about how to deal with liabilities. Remember we called it debt. Debt must be a target to eliminate not to increase. I believe that you have learned a great deal in this book to eliminate and minimize liability. Now, if you have jumped around in the book, I am sorry, you must go back. Any successful wealth building campaign will demand consistency. Plan and remain focused on your goals. You can do it. To reflect back on what liabilities are, go to Chapter Two.

SECURING AND DEVELOPING ASSETS

This is the final section of knowledge that I hope will finalize your development. Building wealth is within your confinements already, but you must develop them to receive its benefits. *"Your fulfillments are within the boundary of your disadvantage and disabilities."* What I am trying to share with you is simply this; you have the resources to get wealth everyday. To secure it, you must use all of the principles that you have learned. Your foundation should not only consist of money, but, also of knowledge.

I really recommend that you go back and reread chapter one. This chapter offers you the principles that you will need. I cannot say how important it is use to these principles as you make your decisions. The process of making sound judgment has the largest impact on any growth that you may receive.

All throughout this book, we talked about primarily seven thing that allows you a true opportunity to unlock your wealth. As you reflect on what you have learned and apply it to your financial situation, you should now identify higher standards as you manage your finances. Just getting through setting up a budget and finally achieving some goals can be exhausting and you simply think that it is over. But, it is really a point and time that you can develop new goals, or get your doubting partner to come aboard.

As you control your expenses, you can increase your ability to develop wealth. A properly used budget can also be used to control the amount of liabilities you take on in the future. If you are truly organized with the management of your money, you will be fully prepared to justify all of your decisions. Sound judgment is so very important when you make financial decisions. As you move forward with the management of money, remember that it is your **power over money. The definition of power is the capacity and the ability, to act and perform effectively.**

DEVELOPING WEALTH

Accumulating wealth is a commitment that you will have to make. In this section I hope to create a thirst for commitment. Once you understand the process of compound interest, you have found one of the keys to unlock wealth.

I was giving a weekly seminar to a group of police officers, when one of them gave me the concept of using 100% compound interest. He stated that he read somewhere that you can take a penny and double it, and the next day double what you had the day before for thirty days. If you did so, you would have over $2,000,000.00 in thirty days. No way, right? I was wrong and it is true. However, it was not realist for the average individual.

Therefore, I began to see how one could make it a reality. What if you used the same concept but over 30 weeks, months, or even years? Instead of using 100% compound interest, what about 10% or 20%? Could you do it? I think so. With the right commitment, maybe you can set a goal for $200,000.00 in 30 months.

Regardless of how much you begin with or set your goal for, just get started. That penny theory did not include interest. It was all principle. Imagine 15% interest compounding on that money. Wow!

Look at compound interest in this manner as well. Take two students in their first year of college, they both agree that they would like to invest one day. Student number 1 decides that he will begin to save a thousand dollars a year until he graduates. The other decided that he would wait until after he graduates. For six years student number 1 saved $6,000.00 with a return of 10% each year and will receive 10% for the next 34 years. Also, he will not add any more money into his investment. Student number 2 started saving a thousand dollars right after he graduated. He invested $34,000.00 over 34 years and also received 10% return each year, but he will never catch student number 1. Why is that? Time value on money. That is what compounding can do for you. So, begin now.

Finally, what you have learned is my seven principles of unlocking wealth. If you go back and think of what you have learned, and the impact that it can make in your financial life, the burden is on you, not products or services. We hope to have sharpened your skills, and crave a new way to manage your money and create wealth. Below are the seven principle that you can master.

Biblical Principles - Understanding God's foundation in dealing with money and that our ability to get wealth is by His power.

Sound Judgment - Using the foundation of biblical principles to make judgment.

Determine Goals - Your ability to use sound judgment to establish your goals.

Budgeting - Managing your goals with control.

Relationship - Understanding the need of a sound relationship with your money and your bank.

Eliminate Liability - The need to reduce debt simply by understanding the processes of the accumulation of interest.

Secure and Develop Assets - Knowing what assets are and the need to develop them as you eliminate debt. Securing it with foundation products.

By sharing this information with your immediate family you will help unlock and break the generational curses that plague many families. You now have the keys use them effectively.

AREAS TO DEVELOP

Income
1. Analyze how personal choices, education/training, technology, and other factors affect future income.
2. Identify sources of income, including entrepreneurial activity.
3. Learn how tax policies, personal taxes, and transfer payments affect disposable income.

Spending
1. Compare the advantages and disadvantages of spending now and spending later.
2. Evaluate the benefits and costs of using different transaction instruments, such as cash, checking accounts, debit cards, credit cards, money orders, electronic fund transfers, and other financial services.
3. Learn how the risk level of the borrower affects the price of credit.
4. Understand how payment performance determines credit history and why these records are maintained and accessed.
5. Learn the rights and responsibilities of buyers, sellers, and creditors under various consumer protection laws.
6. Use cost-benefit analysis to choose among spending alternatives, such as housing, transportation.
7. Identify and analyze pros and cons of alternative action to deal with credit over extension or other financial difficulties.

Money Management

1. Identify the cost of a financial decision as it applies to income, spending, and saving.
2. Establish and evaluate short and long- term financial goals and plans regarding income, spending, saving, and investing.
3. Develop, analyze and revise a budget.
4. Understand relationships with taxes, spending, and investing.
5. Develop a risk management plan that includes life, automobile, property, health, and income protection/ disability insurance.
6. Develop personal financial responsibility.

Perform basic financial operations, such as using checking and savings accounts.

Saving

1. Establish a checking and savings account.
2. Establish a systematic savings plans.
3. Learn about mutual fund accounts.
4. Look into certificate of deposits (CD's).
5. Understand the need for insurance.
6. Identify and analyze the degree of risk in stocks, bonds, and individual retirement accounts.

Saving and Investing

1. Compare the advantages and disadvantages of saving or investing now and later.
2. Explain the importance of short and long-term savings and investment strategies.
3. Identify and evaluate the risk, return, and liquidity of various savings and investment instruments in a number of household circumstances.
4. Explain how taxes, government policy/regulation, and inflation impact savings and investment decisions.

IMPORTANT DEFINITIONS

Adjustable Rate - An interest rate, which can be periodically adjusted up or down, usually in response to, changes in the prime rate. Also called variable rate or floating rate. opposite of fixed rate.

Adverse Information - Information that will cause a credit application to be declined or restricted according to a creditor's policy.

Alternative Credit History - Known as "non-traditional credit." Established credit sources that do not typically appear on a credit report, i.e., past and present rental payments, utility payments, telephone bill payments, monthly insurance payments, etc. Any source which can be documented, where payments have been made on a timely basis.

Annual Percentage Rate (APR) - The yearly cost of a mortgage, including interest, mortgage insurance, and the origination fee (points), expressed as a percentage.

Asset - An item of one's property or the value of property owned.

Average Monthly Payment - The minimum monthly payment required on a credit account.

Balance - The amount left to be paid on the loan or charge card. More precisely, it is the difference between the total amount borrowed and the amount already paid back.

Balance Sheet - A statement of financial conditions as of a specific date. It is different from a cash flow statement, which summarizes income and expenses.

Bank Credit Card - A credit card issued by a bank offering a line of credit and enabling the borrower to make purchases or obtain a cash loan.

Bankruptcy - A proceeding in the federal or provincial court whereby a person who is unable to pay his debts in full may be discharged from the legal obligation to do so.

Bankruptcy Code - The body of a federal statutory law that governs the bankruptcy process.

Bankruptcy Petition - The legal instrument filed with the bankruptcy court that commences a bankruptcy proceeding.

Chapter 7 - In a Chapter 7 proceeding, the debtor's business is liquidated and its assets are distributed to creditors with allowed proof of claims.

Chapter 11 - Normally, a Chapter 11 proceeding is a reorganization proceeding. The debtor continues to operate its business after the bankruptcy is filed. Chapter 11 liquidation is commonplace and usually results from an unsuccessful reorganization attempt.

Chapter 11 Plan - In a Chapter 11 proceeding, the reorganization plan sets forth the rights of all classes of creditors. It may also include various repayment schedules pertaining to the various creditors.

Chapter 13 - May only be filed by an individual debtor with limited debt. In essence, it allows a payment plan for an individual or business debts.

Closing - When a bankruptcy case is closed, it is no longer on the court's docket.

Collateral - Property of a debtor in which a creditor has a lien securing its debt.

Collection Account - Refers to the status of an account owed to a creditor when it has been transferred the debt to a Collection Department either of the creditor's firm or to a separate professional debt collecting firm.

Complaint - A pleading that is filed to initiate a lawsuit, an adversary proceeding.

Consumer Credit - Non-profit organizations designed to help debtors Counseling Services make payment arrangements with creditors.

Consumer Statement - A 100 word or less statement, written by you, explaining the situation on a particular disputed item on your credit file.

Conversion - Changing a bankruptcy case from one chapter type to another.

Credit History - Record of how a consumer has paid charge accounts in the past, as a guide to whether he/she is likely to pay accounts on time in the future.

Credit Inquiry - A request from a person or firm for a credit report. These are customarily listed on the credit file and become a part of it for two years.

Credit Investigation - A Term used in Section 611 of the Federal Fair Credit Reporting Act "Procedure in case of Disputed Accuracy." When a dispute is registered by a consumer about the accuracy of an item in the file, the credit reporting agency is obligated (with some exceptions) to re-check the information with the person or creditor which contributed it. When disputed information cannot be verified it must be deleted.

Creditor - One to whom you owe money.

Debtor - One who owes debts. In bankruptcy, the bank business that is under the control and protection of the bankruptcy court is the debtor.

Deletion - Removal of an item from the credit file.

Derogatory Credit - Negative credit ratings that detract from the overall character of a credit profile.

Discharge - A discharge in bankruptcy relieves the debtor of the discharge able debts incurred prior to filing. Discharge is the legal term for the elimination of debt through bankruptcy.

Disclosure - Explanation of contents of a credit file to a consumer in accordance with the Fair Credit Reporting Act. The Act provides for disclosure by either personal review or telephone. Many credit bureaus offer a copy of the credit file to you in lieu of these other means of disclosure.

Dismissal - The dismissal of a bankruptcy case, for all intents and purposes, returns the debtor to the same place it was before bankruptcy was filed.

Equifax - One of the three major credit reporting agencies, (Equifax is the abbreviated old name for Equifax credit reporting division, the new name is Equifax Credit Information Services).

Examiner - An officer of the court sometimes appointed to investigate the financial affairs of the debtor.

Exemption/Exempt Property - Property of an individual debtor that the law protects from the actions of creditors, such as the debtor's residence or homestead, automobile and the like.

Experian - One of the three major credit reporting agencies.

Fixed-Rate - A loan in which the interest rate does not change during the entire term of the loan. opposite of adjustable rate.

Foreclosure - A debt -collection procedure whereby property of the debtor is sold to satisfy debts. Foreclosure often involves real estate of the debtor.

General, Unsecured Claim - A claim that is neither secured nor granted a priority by the Bankruptcy Code. Most trade debts are general, unsecured claims.

Installment Credit Account - A credit account in which the amount of the payment, and the number of payments is pre-determined of fixed.

Interest Rate - Interest per year divided by principal amount, expressed as a percentage.

Involuntary Bankruptcy - In an involuntary bankruptcy proceeding the debtors is forced into bankruptcy by creditors. Involuntary bankruptcies are rare.

Joint Account - Loan or charge account where two parties, usually spouses, are responsible for the debts, as distinguished from an individual account.

Judicial Lien - A lien created by the order of a court, such as the lien created by taking a judgment against a debtor.

Jurisdiction - The power and authority of a court to issue binding orders after hearing controversies.

Levy and Execution - A judicial debt-collection procedure in which the court orders the sheriff to seize the debtor's property found in the county to sell in satisfaction of the debtor's debt or debts.

Lien - An interest in property securing the repayment of a debt.

Motion - A request for the court to act. A motion may be filed within a law-suit, adversary proceeding or bankruptcy case.

Past Due Account - An account where the payment is overdue.

Payment Term - The time frame in which you has agreed to pay off a debt.

Personal Property - Moveable property. Property that is not permanently attached to land is considered personality.

Petition for Relief - The papers filed initiating a bankruptcy case.

Possessory Security Interest - A security interest or lien on property that requires the creditor to have possession of the property, such as a pawn or pledge.

Prime Rate - The interest rate that commercial banks charge their most creditworthy borrowers, such as large corporations. The prime rate is a lagging indicator. also called prime.

Priority - the Bankruptcy Code, such as claims for lost wages or taxes, designates certain categories of claims as priority claims. Each classification of claims must be paid in order of priority(the claims in one class must be paid in full before the next class receives any payment.

Proof of Claim - The document filed in bankruptcy case that establishes a creditor's claim for payment against the debtor.

Public Record - Information obtained by the credit bureau from court records, e.g., liens, bankruptcy filings and judgments. Called "public record" because the files containing this data are open to any person who requests to see them.

Realty or Real Property - Immovable property, such as land and/or buildings attached to land.

Redemption - The right of a debtor in a bankruptcy to purchase property from a secured creditor by paying the current value of the property (regardless of the amount owed on the property).

Reported Date - Date that an account or information on an account, was reported to the credit bureau.

Repossession - Forced or voluntary surrender of a financed item of personal property(such as a car or furniture) as a result of the customer's failure to pay as promised.

Revolving Credit Accounts - A credit agreement that provides a line of credit up to a set limit, with the choice of paying in full at the end of each billing period, or paying over several billing periods with a finance charge applied on the unpaid balance.

Rule of 72 - The estimation of doubling time on an investment, for which the compounded annual rate of return times the number of years must equal roughly 72 for the investment to double in value.

Rule of 78 - A formula used to determine rebates on interest for installment loans; since $1 + 2 + ... + 12 = 78$, 1/78th of the interest is owed after the first month, 3/78ths after the second month, etc.

Secured Credit Card - A credit card secured by a savings account that has been established in advance by the borrower. The amount in the account usually determines the limit on the credit card. These accounts present no real risk factor for creditors.

Secured Creditor - A creditors debt secured by a lien on property of the debtor.

Security Interest - A lien on the property in the possession of the debtor that acts as security for the debt owed to the creditor.

Settlement - An agreement reached between the creditor and an individual regarding an outstanding balance.

Simple Interest - The interest calculated on a principal sum, not compounded on earned interest.

Statutory Lien - A lien created by operation of law, such as a mechanic's lien/ tax lien. A statutory lien does not require the consent of the parties/a court order.

Times Past Due - A section on the credit report that reflects a history of the number of times a consumer has paid late on an account.

Trade Line - A credit account described in the credit history of a credit file.

Trans Union - One of the three major credit reporting agencies.

Trustee - An officer of the court appointed to take custody of the assets of a bankruptcy estate.

Updated Report - A credit report which shows the most recent status of all the information recorded on the file about a consumer.

Unsecured Creditor - A creditor without security for its debt.

IMPORTANT INFORMATION

There is a lot of information available that is free to you, as a consumer. I would recommend that you get that information and use it. After all, your credit is your life. The Federal Trade Commission provides information about credit that will help in guiding you. They also provide enforcement of the laws, which govern credit and you.

The Laws:
The Equal Credit Opportunity Act
The Fair Credit Reporting Act
The Truth In Lending Act
The Fair Credit Billing Act
The Fair Debt Collection Practices Act

The Publications:
Building a Better Credit Report
Credit and Divorce
Fair Credit Reporting
Fair Debt Collection
Solving Credit Problems

Call (202)326-2222 or Write: Federal Trade Commission,
Washington, D. C. 20580

ADDRESSES FOR CREDIT REPORTING AGENCY

Equifax Credit Inf. Service	Trans Union Corp.	Experian
P. O. Box 740256	P. O. Box 2000	P. O. Box 949
Atlanta, GA 30374	Chester, PA. 19022-2000	Chatsworth, CA 91313
(800)291-7773	(800)916-8800	(800)583-4080